THIS IS YOUR **PASSBOOK**® FOR ...

TAXPAYER SERVICE REPRESENTATIVE

NATIONAL LEARNING CORPORATION®
passbooks.com

PASSBOOK® SERIES

THE *PASSBOOK® SERIES* has been created to prepare applicants and candidates for the ultimate academic battlefield – the examination room.

At some time in our lives, each and every one of us may be required to take an examination – for validation, matriculation, admission, qualification, registration, certification, or licensure.

Based on the assumption that every applicant or candidate has met the basic formal educational standards, has taken the required number of courses, and read the necessary texts, the *PASSBOOK® SERIES* furnishes the one special preparation which may assure passing with confidence, instead of failing with insecurity. Examination questions – together with answers – are furnished as the basic vehicle for study so that the mysteries of the examination and its compounding difficulties may be eliminated or diminished by a sure method.

This book is meant to help you pass your examination provided that you qualify and are serious in your objective.

The entire field is reviewed through the huge store of content information which is succinctly presented through a provocative and challenging approach – the question-and-answer method.

A climate of success is established by furnishing the correct answers at the end of each test.

You soon learn to recognize types of questions, forms of questions, and patterns of questioning. You may even begin to anticipate expected outcomes.

You perceive that many questions are repeated or adapted so that you can gain acute insights, which may enable you to score many sure points.

You learn how to confront new questions, or types of questions, and to attack them confidently and work out the correct answers.

You note objectives and emphases, and recognize pitfalls and dangers, so that you may make positive educational adjustments.

Moreover, you are kept fully informed in relation to new concepts, methods, practices, and directions in the field.

You discover that you arre actually taking the examination all the time: you are preparing for the examination by "taking" an examination, not by reading extraneous and/or supererogatory textbooks.

In short, this PASSBOOK®, used directedly, should be an important factor in helping you to pass your test.

TAXPAYER SERVICES REPRESENTATIVE

Duties

As a Taxpayer Services Representative I under the supervision of a Taxpayer Services Representative II, you would work in an environment using the latest technology and automated operations to provide information and assistance to the taxpaying public. You would answer taxpayers' or tax practitioners' questions by telephone, by letter, or in person concerning the provisions and requirements of the Tax Law administered by the Department; assist taxpayers in their preparation of Corporation, Income, Miscellaneous, and Sales Tax Returns; and assist taxpayers in their computation of taxes, penalties, and interest due the State. You would assist the public in the completion of all applications for licenses and registration forms and prepare written responses to requests for information. You would research Tax Department computer data files using a variety of software applications and provide explanations for account and refund adjustments, verify payments, and update taxpayer account information. You might issue taxpayer registrations, handle changes in registrations, and respond to taxpayers' inquiries regarding assessments, including explaining the reasons for assessments, and follow-up to resolve taxpayers' problems. You would research Tax Laws and Regulations in the more commonly used reference materials such as tax law publications, attend periodic training sessions to upgrade technical skills, and assist in training seasonal Tax Information Aides. You would be expected to act in a calm, courteous, and reasonable manner even under very difficult, highly stressful, and at times, confrontational circumstances. When assigned to a call center, you would wear a headset and would answer telephone calls which are automatically and continuously distributed by a complex telephonic system. This system does not allow for breaks between calls; when one caller disconnects, another call is automatically routed to the Taxpayer Services Representative. You would be expected to effectively use the telephone system and associated computer software. Telephone calls may be monitored for quality assurance.

SUBJECT OF EXAMINATION

The written test is designed to test for knowledge, skills, and/or abilities in such areas as:
1. Evaluating conclusions in light of known facts;
2. Preparing written material;
3. Public contact principles and practices;
4. Understanding and interpreting tabular material; and
5. Understanding and interpreting written material.

HOW TO TAKE A TEST

I. YOU MUST PASS AN EXAMINATION

A. *WHAT EVERY CANDIDATE SHOULD KNOW*

Examination applicants often ask us for help in preparing for the written test. What can I study in advance? What kinds of questions will be asked? How will the test be given? How will the papers be graded?

As an applicant for a civil service examination, you may be wondering about some of these things. Our purpose here is to suggest effective methods of advance study and to describe civil service examinations.

Your chances for success on this examination can be increased if you know how to prepare. Those "pre-examination jitters" can be reduced if you know what to expect. You can even experience an adventure in good citizenship if you know why civil service exams are given.

B. *WHY ARE CIVIL SERVICE EXAMINATIONS GIVEN?*

Civil service examinations are important to you in two ways. As a citizen, you want public jobs filled by employees who know how to do their work. As a job seeker, you want a fair chance to compete for that job on an equal footing with other candidates. The best-known means of accomplishing this two-fold goal is the competitive examination.

Exams are widely publicized throughout the nation. They may be administered for jobs in federal, state, city, municipal, town or village governments or agencies.

Any citizen may apply, with some limitations, such as the age or residence of applicants. Your experience and education may be reviewed to see whether you meet the requirements for the particular examination. When these requirements exist, they are reasonable and applied consistently to all applicants. Thus, a competitive examination may cause you some uneasiness now, but it is your privilege and safeguard.

C. *HOW ARE CIVIL SERVICE EXAMS DEVELOPED?*

Examinations are carefully written by trained technicians who are specialists in the field known as "psychological measurement," in consultation with recognized authorities in the field of work that the test will cover. These experts recommend the subject matter areas or skills to be tested; only those knowledges or skills important to your success on the job are included. The most reliable books and source materials available are used as references. Together, the experts and technicians judge the difficulty level of the questions.

Test technicians know how to phrase questions so that the problem is clearly stated. Their ethics do not permit "trick" or "catch" questions. Questions may have been tried out on sample groups, or subjected to statistical analysis, to determine their usefulness.

Written tests are often used in combination with performance tests, ratings of training and experience, and oral interviews. All of these measures combine to form the best-known means of finding the right person for the right job.

II. HOW TO PASS THE WRITTEN TEST

A. NATURE OF THE EXAMINATION

To prepare intelligently for civil service examinations, you should know how they differ from school examinations you have taken. In school you were assigned certain definite pages to read or subjects to cover. The examination questions were quite detailed and usually emphasized memory. Civil service exams, on the other hand, try to discover your present ability to perform the duties of a position, plus your potentiality to learn these duties. In other words, a civil service exam attempts to predict how successful you will be. Questions cover such a broad area that they cannot be as minute and detailed as school exam questions.

In the public service similar kinds of work, or positions, are grouped together in one "class." This process is known as *position-classification*. All the positions in a class are paid according to the salary range for that class. One class title covers all of these positions, and they are all tested by the same examination.

B. FOUR BASIC STEPS

1) Study the announcement

How, then, can you know what subjects to study? Our best answer is: "Learn as much as possible about the class of positions for which you've applied." The exam will test the knowledge, skills and abilities needed to do the work.

Your most valuable source of information about the position you want is the official exam announcement. This announcement lists the training and experience qualifications. Check these standards and apply only if you come reasonably close to meeting them.

The brief description of the position in the examination announcement offers some clues to the subjects which will be tested. Think about the job itself. Review the duties in your mind. Can you perform them, or are there some in which you are rusty? Fill in the blank spots in your preparation.

Many jurisdictions preview the written test in the exam announcement by including a section called "Knowledge and Abilities Required," "Scope of the Examination," or some similar heading. Here you will find out specifically what fields will be tested.

2) Review your own background

Once you learn in general what the position is all about, and what you need to know to do the work, ask yourself which subjects you already know fairly well and which need improvement. You may wonder whether to concentrate on improving your strong areas or on building some background in your fields of weakness. When the announcement has specified "some knowledge" or "considerable knowledge," or has used adjectives like "beginning principles of..." or "advanced ... methods," you can get a clue as to the number and difficulty of questions to be asked in any given field. More questions, and hence broader coverage, would be included for those subjects which are more important in the work. Now weigh your strengths and weaknesses against the job requirements and prepare accordingly.

3) **Determine the level of the position**

Another way to tell how intensively you should prepare is to understand the level of the job for which you are applying. Is it the entering level? In other words, is this the position in which beginners in a field of work are hired? Or is it an intermediate or advanced level? Sometimes this is indicated by such words as "Junior" or "Senior" in the class title. Other jurisdictions use Roman numerals to designate the level – Clerk I, Clerk II, for example. The word "Supervisor" sometimes appears in the title. If the level is not indicated by the title, check the description of duties. Will you be working under very close supervision, or will you have responsibility for independent decisions in this work?

4) **Choose appropriate study materials**

Now that you know the subjects to be examined and the relative amount of each subject to be covered, you can choose suitable study materials. For beginning level jobs, or even advanced ones, if you have a pronounced weakness in some aspect of your training, read a modern, standard textbook in that field. Be sure it is up to date and has general coverage. Such books are normally available at your library, and the librarian will be glad to help you locate one. For entry-level positions, questions of appropriate difficulty are chosen – neither highly advanced questions, nor those too simple. Such questions require careful thought but not advanced training.

If the position for which you are applying is technical or advanced, you will read more advanced, specialized material. If you are already familiar with the basic principles of your field, elementary textbooks would waste your time. Concentrate on advanced textbooks and technical periodicals. Think through the concepts and review difficult problems in your field.

These are all general sources. You can get more ideas on your own initiative, following these leads. For example, training manuals and publications of the government agency which employs workers in your field can be useful, particularly for technical and professional positions. A letter or visit to the government department involved may result in more specific study suggestions, and certainly will provide you with a more definite idea of the exact nature of the position you are seeking.

III. KINDS OF TESTS

Tests are used for purposes other than measuring knowledge and ability to perform specified duties. For some positions, it is equally important to test ability to make adjustments to new situations or to profit from training. In others, basic mental abilities not dependent on information are essential. Questions which test these things may not appear as pertinent to the duties of the position as those which test for knowledge and information. Yet they are often highly important parts of a fair examination. For very general questions, it is almost impossible to help you direct your study efforts. What we can do is to point out some of the more common of these general abilities needed in public service positions and describe some typical questions.

1) General information

Broad, general information has been found useful for predicting job success in some kinds of work. This is tested in a variety of ways, from vocabulary lists to questions about current events. Basic background in some field of work, such as sociology or economics, may be sampled in a group of questions. Often these are principles which have become familiar to most persons through exposure rather than through formal training. It is difficult to advise you how to study for these questions; being alert to the world around you is our best suggestion.

2) Verbal ability

An example of an ability needed in many positions is verbal or language ability. Verbal ability is, in brief, the ability to use and understand words. Vocabulary and grammar tests are typical measures of this ability. Reading comprehension or paragraph interpretation questions are common in many kinds of civil service tests. You are given a paragraph of written material and asked to find its central meaning.

3) Numerical ability

Number skills can be tested by the familiar arithmetic problem, by checking paired lists of numbers to see which are alike and which are different, or by interpreting charts and graphs. In the latter test, a graph may be printed in the test booklet which you are asked to use as the basis for answering questions.

4) Observation

A popular test for law-enforcement positions is the observation test. A picture is shown to you for several minutes, then taken away. Questions about the picture test your ability to observe both details and larger elements.

5) Following directions

In many positions in the public service, the employee must be able to carry out written instructions dependably and accurately. You may be given a chart with several columns, each column listing a variety of information. The questions require you to carry out directions involving the information given in the chart.

6) Skills and aptitudes

Performance tests effectively measure some manual skills and aptitudes. When the skill is one in which you are trained, such as typing or shorthand, you can practice. These tests are often very much like those given in business school or high school courses. For many of the other skills and aptitudes, however, no short-time preparation can be made. Skills and abilities natural to you or that you have developed throughout your lifetime are being tested.

Many of the general questions just described provide all the data needed to answer the questions and ask you to use your reasoning ability to find the answers. Your best preparation for these tests, as well as for tests of facts and ideas, is to be at your physical and mental best. You, no doubt, have your own methods of getting into an exam-taking mood and keeping "in shape." The next section lists some ideas on this subject.

IV. KINDS OF QUESTIONS

Only rarely is the "essay" question, which you answer in narrative form, used in civil service tests. Civil service tests are usually of the short-answer type. Full instructions for answering these questions will be given to you at the examination. But in case this is your first experience with short-answer questions and separate answer sheets, here is what you need to know:

1) Multiple-choice Questions

Most popular of the short-answer questions is the "multiple choice" or "best answer" question. It can be used, for example, to test for factual knowledge, ability to solve problems or judgment in meeting situations found at work.

A multiple-choice question is normally one of three types—

- It can begin with an incomplete statement followed by several possible endings. You are to find the one ending which *best* completes the statement, although some of the others may not be entirely wrong.
- It can also be a complete statement in the form of a question which is answered by choosing one of the statements listed.
- It can be in the form of a problem – again you select the best answer.

Here is an example of a multiple-choice question with a discussion which should give you some clues as to the method for choosing the right answer:

When an employee has a complaint about his assignment, the action which will *best* help him overcome his difficulty is to
  A. discuss his difficulty with his coworkers
  B. take the problem to the head of the organization
  C. take the problem to the person who gave him the assignment
  D. say nothing to anyone about his complaint

In answering this question, you should study each of the choices to find which is best. Consider choice "A" – Certainly an employee may discuss his complaint with fellow employees, but no change or improvement can result, and the complaint remains unresolved. Choice "B" is a poor choice since the head of the organization probably does not know what assignment you have been given, and taking your problem to him is known as "going over the head" of the supervisor. The supervisor, or person who made the assignment, is the person who can clarify it or correct any injustice. Choice "C" is, therefore, correct. To say nothing, as in choice "D," is unwise. Supervisors have and interest in knowing the problems employees are facing, and the employee is seeking a solution to his problem.

2) True/False Questions

The "true/false" or "right/wrong" form of question is sometimes used. Here a complete statement is given. Your job is to decide whether the statement is right or wrong.

SAMPLE: A roaming cell-phone call to a nearby city costs less than a non-roaming call to a distant city.

This statement is wrong, or false, since roaming calls are more expensive.
This is not a complete list of all possible question forms, although most of the others are variations of these common types. You will always get complete directions for

answering questions. Be sure you understand *how* to mark your answers – ask questions until you do.

V. RECORDING YOUR ANSWERS

Computer terminals are used more and more today for many different kinds of exams.

For an examination with very few applicants, you may be told to record your answers in the test booklet itself. Separate answer sheets are much more common. If this separate answer sheet is to be scored by machine – and this is often the case – it is highly important that you mark your answers correctly in order to get credit.

An electronic scoring machine is often used in civil service offices because of the speed with which papers can be scored. Machine-scored answer sheets must be marked with a pencil, which will be given to you. This pencil has a high graphite content which responds to the electronic scoring machine. As a matter of fact, stray dots may register as answers, so do not let your pencil rest on the answer sheet while you are pondering the correct answer. Also, if your pencil lead breaks or is otherwise defective, ask for another.

Since the answer sheet will be dropped in a slot in the scoring machine, be careful not to bend the corners or get the paper crumpled.

The answer sheet normally has five vertical columns of numbers, with 30 numbers to a column. These numbers correspond to the question numbers in your test booklet. After each number, going across the page are four or five pairs of dotted lines. These short dotted lines have small letters or numbers above them. The first two pairs may also have a "T" or "F" above the letters. This indicates that the first two pairs only are to be used if the questions are of the true-false type. If the questions are multiple choice, disregard the "T" and "F" and pay attention only to the small letters or numbers.

Answer your questions in the manner of the sample that follows:

> 32. The largest city in the United States is
>> A. Washington, D.C.
>> B. New York City
>> C. Chicago
>> D. Detroit
>> E. San Francisco

> 1) Choose the answer you think is best. (New York City is the largest, so "B" is correct.)
> 2) Find the row of dotted lines numbered the same as the question you are answering. (Find row number 32)
> 3) Find the pair of dotted lines corresponding to the answer. (Find the pair of lines under the mark "B.")
> 4) Make a solid black mark between the dotted lines.

VI. BEFORE THE TEST

Common sense will help you find procedures to follow to get ready for an examination. Too many of us, however, overlook these sensible measures. Indeed, nervousness and fatigue have been found to be the most serious reasons why applicants fail to do their best on civil service tests. Here is a list of reminders:

- Begin your preparation early – Don't wait until the last minute to go scurrying around for books and materials or to find out what the position is all about.
- Prepare continuously – An hour a night for a week is better than an all-night cram session. This has been definitely established. What is more, a night a week for a month will return better dividends than crowding your study into a shorter period of time.
- Locate the place of the exam – You have been sent a notice telling you when and where to report for the examination. If the location is in a different town or otherwise unfamiliar to you, it would be well to inquire the best route and learn something about the building.
- Relax the night before the test – Allow your mind to rest. Do not study at all that night. Plan some mild recreation or diversion; then go to bed early and get a good night's sleep.
- Get up early enough to make a leisurely trip to the place for the test – This way unforeseen events, traffic snarls, unfamiliar buildings, etc. will not upset you.
- Dress comfortably – A written test is not a fashion show. You will be known by number and not by name, so wear something comfortable.
- Leave excess paraphernalia at home – Shopping bags and odd bundles will get in your way. You need bring only the items mentioned in the official notice you received; usually everything you need is provided. Do not bring reference books to the exam. They will only confuse those last minutes and be taken away from you when in the test room.
- Arrive somewhat ahead of time – If because of transportation schedules you must get there very early, bring a newspaper or magazine to take your mind off yourself while waiting.
- Locate the examination room – When you have found the proper room, you will be directed to the seat or part of the room where you will sit. Sometimes you are given a sheet of instructions to read while you are waiting. Do not fill out any forms until you are told to do so; just read them and be prepared.
- Relax and prepare to listen to the instructions
- If you have any physical problem that may keep you from doing your best, be sure to tell the test administrator. If you are sick or in poor health, you really cannot do your best on the exam. You can come back and take the test some other time.

VII. AT THE TEST

The day of the test is here and you have the test booklet in your hand. The temptation to get going is very strong. Caution! There is more to success than knowing the right answers. You must know how to identify your papers and understand variations in the type of short-answer question used in this particular examination. Follow these suggestions for maximum results from your efforts:

1) Cooperate with the monitor

The test administrator has a duty to create a situation in which you can be as much at ease as possible. He will give instructions, tell you when to begin, check to see that you are marking your answer sheet correctly, and so on. He is not there to guard you, although he will see that your competitors do not take unfair advantage. He wants to help you do your best.

2) Listen to all instructions

Don't jump the gun! Wait until you understand all directions. In most civil service tests you get more time than you need to answer the questions. So don't be in a hurry. Read each word of instructions until you clearly understand the meaning. Study the examples, listen to all announcements and follow directions. Ask questions if you do not understand what to do.

3) Identify your papers

Civil service exams are usually identified by number only. You will be assigned a number; you must not put your name on your test papers. Be sure to copy your number correctly. Since more than one exam may be given, copy your exact examination title.

4) Plan your time

Unless you are told that a test is a "speed" or "rate of work" test, speed itself is usually not important. Time enough to answer all the questions will be provided, but this does not mean that you have all day. An overall time limit has been set. Divide the total time (in minutes) by the number of questions to determine the approximate time you have for each question.

5) Do not linger over difficult questions

If you come across a difficult question, mark it with a paper clip (useful to have along) and come back to it when you have been through the booklet. One caution if you do this – be sure to skip a number on your answer sheet as well. Check often to be sure that you have not lost your place and that you are marking in the row numbered the same as the question you are answering.

6) Read the questions

Be sure you know what the question asks! Many capable people are unsuccessful because they failed to *read* the questions correctly.

7) Answer all questions

Unless you have been instructed that a penalty will be deducted for incorrect answers, it is better to guess than to omit a question.

8) Speed tests

It is often better NOT to guess on speed tests. It has been found that on timed tests people are tempted to spend the last few seconds before time is called in marking answers at random – without even reading them – in the hope of picking up a few extra points. To discourage this practice, the instructions may warn you that your score will be "corrected" for guessing. That is, a penalty will be applied. The incorrect answers will be deducted from the correct ones, or some other penalty formula will be used.

9) Review your answers

If you finish before time is called, go back to the questions you guessed or omitted to give them further thought. Review other answers if you have time.

10) Return your test materials

If you are ready to leave before others have finished or time is called, take ALL your materials to the monitor and leave quietly. Never take any test material with you. The monitor can discover whose papers are not complete, and taking a test booklet may be grounds for disqualification.

VIII. EXAMINATION TECHNIQUES

1) Read the general instructions carefully. These are usually printed on the first page of the exam booklet. As a rule, these instructions refer to the timing of the examination; the fact that you should not start work until the signal and must stop work at a signal, etc. If there are any *special* instructions, such as a choice of questions to be answered, make sure that you note this instruction carefully.

2) When you are ready to start work on the examination, that is as soon as the signal has been given, read the instructions to each question booklet, underline any key words or phrases, such as *least, best, outline, describe* and the like. In this way you will tend to answer as requested rather than discover on reviewing your paper that you *listed without describing*, that you selected the *worst* choice rather than the *best* choice, etc.

3) If the examination is of the objective or multiple-choice type – that is, each question will also give a series of possible answers: A, B, C or D, and you are called upon to select the best answer and write the letter next to that answer on your answer paper – it is advisable to start answering each question in turn. There may be anywhere from 50 to 100 such questions in the three or four hours allotted and you can see how much time would be taken if you read through all the questions before beginning to answer any. Furthermore, if you come across a question or group of questions which you know would be difficult to answer, it would undoubtedly affect your handling of all the other questions.

4) If the examination is of the essay type and contains but a few questions, it is a moot point as to whether you should read all the questions before starting to answer any one. Of course, if you are given a choice – say five out of seven and the like – then it is essential to read all the questions so you can eliminate the two that are most difficult. If, however, you are asked to answer all the questions, there may be danger in trying to answer the easiest one first because you may find that you will spend too much time on it. The best technique is to answer the first question, then proceed to the second, etc.

5) Time your answers. Before the exam begins, write down the time it started, then add the time allowed for the examination and write down the time it must be completed, then divide the time available somewhat as follows:

- If 3-1/2 hours are allowed, that would be 210 minutes. If you have 80 objective-type questions, that would be an average of 2-1/2 minutes per question. Allow yourself no more than 2 minutes per question, or a total of 160 minutes, which will permit about 50 minutes to review.
- If for the time allotment of 210 minutes there are 7 essay questions to answer, that would average about 30 minutes a question. Give yourself only 25 minutes per question so that you have about 35 minutes to review.

6) The most important instruction is to *read each question* and make sure you know what is wanted. The second most important instruction is to *time yourself properly* so that you answer every question. The third most important instruction is to *answer every question*. Guess if you have to but include something for each question. Remember that you will receive no credit for a blank and will probably receive some credit if you write something in answer to an essay question. If you guess a letter – say "B" for a multiple-choice question – you may have guessed right. If you leave a blank as an answer to a multiple-choice question, the examiners may respect your feelings but it will not add a point to your score. Some exams may penalize you for wrong answers, so in such cases *only*, you may not want to guess unless you have some basis for your answer.

7) Suggestions
  a. Objective-type questions
    1. Examine the question booklet for proper sequence of pages and questions
    2. Read all instructions carefully
    3. Skip any question which seems too difficult; return to it after all other questions have been answered
    4. Apportion your time properly; do not spend too much time on any single question or group of questions
    5. Note and underline key words – *all, most, fewest, least, best, worst, same, opposite,* etc.
    6. Pay particular attention to negatives
    7. Note unusual option, e.g., unduly long, short, complex, different or similar in content to the body of the question
    8. Observe the use of "hedging" words – *probably, may, most likely,* etc.
    9. Make sure that your answer is put next to the same number as the question
    10. Do not second-guess unless you have good reason to believe the second answer is definitely more correct
    11. Cross out original answer if you decide another answer is more accurate; do not erase until you are ready to hand your paper in
    12. Answer all questions; guess unless instructed otherwise
    13. Leave time for review

  b. Essay questions
    1. Read each question carefully
    2. Determine exactly what is wanted. Underline key words or phrases.
    3. Decide on outline or paragraph answer

4. Include many different points and elements unless asked to develop any one or two points or elements
5. Show impartiality by giving pros and cons unless directed to select one side only
6. Make and write down any assumptions you find necessary to answer the questions
7. Watch your English, grammar, punctuation and choice of words
8. Time your answers; don't crowd material

8) Answering the essay question

Most essay questions can be answered by framing the specific response around several key words or ideas. Here are a few such key words or ideas:

M's: manpower, materials, methods, money, management
P's: purpose, program, policy, plan, procedure, practice, problems, pitfalls, personnel, public relations
   a. Six basic steps in handling problems:
      1. Preliminary plan and background development
      2. Collect information, data and facts
      3. Analyze and interpret information, data and facts
      4. Analyze and develop solutions as well as make recommendations
      5. Prepare report and sell recommendations
      6. Install recommendations and follow up effectiveness

   b. Pitfalls to avoid
      1. *Taking things for granted* – A statement of the situation does not necessarily imply that each of the elements is necessarily true; for example, a complaint may be invalid and biased so that all that can be taken for granted is that a complaint has been registered
      2. *Considering only one side of a situation* – Wherever possible, indicate several alternatives and then point out the reasons you selected the best one
      3. *Failing to indicate follow up* – Whenever your answer indicates action on your part, make certain that you will take proper follow-up action to see how successful your recommendations, procedures or actions turn out to be
      4. *Taking too long in answering any single question* – Remember to time your answers properly

IX. AFTER THE TEST

Scoring procedures differ in detail among civil service jurisdictions although the general principles are the same. Whether the papers are hand-scored or graded by machine we have described, they are nearly always graded by number. That is, the person who marks the paper knows only the number – never the name – of the applicant. Not until all the papers have been graded will they be matched with names. If other tests, such as training and experience or oral interview ratings have been given, scores will be combined. Different parts of the examination usually have different weights. For example, the written test might count 60 percent of the final grade, and a rating of training and experience 40 percent. In many jurisdictions, veterans will have a certain number of points added to their grades.

After the final grade has been determined, the names are placed in grade order and an eligible list is established. There are various methods for resolving ties between those who get the same final grade – probably the most common is to place first the name of the person whose application was received first. Job offers are made from the eligible list in the order the names appear on it. You will be notified of your grade and your rank as soon as all these computations have been made. This will be done as rapidly as possible.

People who are found to meet the requirements in the announcement are called "eligibles." Their names are put on a list of eligible candidates. An eligible's chances of getting a job depend on how high he stands on this list and how fast agencies are filling jobs from the list.

When a job is to be filled from a list of eligibles, the agency asks for the names of people on the list of eligibles for that job. When the civil service commission receives this request, it sends to the agency the names of the three people highest on this list. Or, if the job to be filled has specialized requirements, the office sends the agency the names of the top three persons who meet these requirements from the general list.

The appointing officer makes a choice from among the three people whose names were sent to him. If the selected person accepts the appointment, the names of the others are put back on the list to be considered for future openings.

That is the rule in hiring from all kinds of eligible lists, whether they are for typist, carpenter, chemist, or something else. For every vacancy, the appointing officer has his choice of any one of the top three eligibles on the list. This explains why the person whose name is on top of the list sometimes does not get an appointment when some of the persons lower on the list do. If the appointing officer chooses the second or third eligible, the No. 1 eligible does not get a job at once, but stays on the list until he is appointed or the list is terminated.

X. HOW TO PASS THE INTERVIEW TEST

The examination for which you applied requires an oral interview test. You have already taken the written test and you are now being called for the interview test – the final part of the formal examination.

You may think that it is not possible to prepare for an interview test and that there are no procedures to follow during an interview. Our purpose is to point out some things you can do in advance that will help you and some good rules to follow and pitfalls to avoid while you are being interviewed.

What is an interview supposed to test?

The written examination is designed to test the technical knowledge and competence of the candidate; the oral is designed to evaluate intangible qualities, not readily measured otherwise, and to establish a list showing the relative fitness of each candidate – as measured against his competitors – for the position sought. Scoring is not on the basis of "right" and "wrong," but on a sliding scale of values ranging from "not passable" to "outstanding." As a matter of fact, it is possible to achieve a relatively low score without a single "incorrect" answer because of evident weakness in the qualities being measured.

Occasionally, an examination may consist entirely of an oral test – either an individual or a group oral. In such cases, information is sought concerning the technical knowledges and abilities of the candidate, since there has been no written examination for this purpose. More commonly, however, an oral test is used to supplement a written examination.

Who conducts interviews?

The composition of oral boards varies among different jurisdictions. In nearly all, a representative of the personnel department serves as chairman. One of the members of the board may be a representative of the department in which the candidate would work. In some cases, "outside experts" are used, and, frequently, a businessman or some other representative of the general public is asked to serve. Labor and management or other special groups may be represented. The aim is to secure the services of experts in the appropriate field.

However the board is composed, it is a good idea (and not at all improper or unethical) to ascertain in advance of the interview who the members are and what groups they represent. When you are introduced to them, you will have some idea of their backgrounds and interests, and at least you will not stutter and stammer over their names.

What should be done before the interview?

While knowledge about the board members is useful and takes some of the surprise element out of the interview, there is other preparation which is more substantive. It *is* possible to prepare for an oral interview – in several ways:

1) Keep a copy of your application and review it carefully before the interview

This may be the only document before the oral board, and the starting point of the interview. Know what education and experience you have listed there, and the sequence and dates of all of it. Sometimes the board will ask you to review the highlights of your experience for them; you should not have to hem and haw doing it.

2) Study the class specification and the examination announcement

Usually, the oral board has one or both of these to guide them. The qualities, characteristics or knowledges required by the position sought are stated in these documents. They offer valuable clues as to the nature of the oral interview. For example, if the job involves supervisory responsibilities, the announcement will usually indicate that knowledge of modern supervisory methods and the qualifications of the candidate as a supervisor will be tested. If so, you can expect such questions, frequently in the form of a hypothetical situation which you are expected to solve. NEVER go into an oral without knowledge of the duties and responsibilities of the job you seek.

3) Think through each qualification required

Try to visualize the kind of questions you would ask if you were a board member. How well could you answer them? Try especially to appraise your own knowledge and background in each area, *measured against the job sought*, and identify any areas in which you are weak. Be critical and realistic – do not flatter yourself.

4) Do some general reading in areas in which you feel you may be weak

For example, if the job involves supervision and your past experience has NOT, some general reading in supervisory methods and practices, particularly in the field of human relations, might be useful. Do NOT study agency procedures or detailed manuals. The oral board will be testing your understanding and capacity, not your memory.

5) Get a good night's sleep and watch your general health and mental attitude

You will want a clear head at the interview. Take care of a cold or any other minor ailment, and of course, no hangovers.

What should be done on the day of the interview?

Now comes the day of the interview itself. Give yourself plenty of time to get there. Plan to arrive somewhat ahead of the scheduled time, particularly if your appointment is in the fore part of the day. If a previous candidate fails to appear, the board might be ready for you a bit early. By early afternoon an oral board is almost invariably behind schedule if there are many candidates, and you may have to wait. Take along a book or magazine to read, or your application to review, but leave any extraneous material in the waiting room when you go in for your interview. In any event, relax and compose yourself.

The matter of dress is important. The board is forming impressions about you – from your experience, your manners, your attitude, and your appearance. Give your personal appearance careful attention. Dress your best, but not your flashiest. Choose conservative, appropriate clothing, and be sure it is immaculate. This is a business interview, and your appearance should indicate that you regard it as such. Besides, being well groomed and properly dressed will help boost your confidence.

Sooner or later, someone will call your name and escort you into the interview room. *This is it.* From here on you are on your own. It is too late for any more preparation. But remember, you asked for this opportunity to prove your fitness, and you are here because your request was granted.

What happens when you go in?

The usual sequence of events will be as follows: The clerk (who is often the board stenographer) will introduce you to the chairman of the oral board, who will introduce you to the other members of the board. Acknowledge the introductions before you sit down. Do not be surprised if you find a microphone facing you or a stenotypist sitting by. Oral interviews are usually recorded in the event of an appeal or other review.

Usually the chairman of the board will open the interview by reviewing the highlights of your education and work experience from your application – primarily for the benefit of the other members of the board, as well as to get the material into the record. Do not interrupt or comment unless there is an error or significant misinterpretation; if that is the case, do not hesitate. But do not quibble about insignificant matters. Also, he will usually ask you some question about your education, experience or your present job – partly to get you to start talking and to establish the interviewing "rapport." He may start the actual questioning, or turn it over to one of the other members. Frequently, each member undertakes the questioning on a particular area, one in which he is perhaps most competent, so you can expect each member to participate in the examination. Because time is limited, you may also expect some rather abrupt switches in the direction the questioning takes, so do not be upset by it. Normally, a board member will not pursue a single line of questioning unless he discovers a particular strength or weakness.

After each member has participated, the chairman will usually ask whether any member has any further questions, then will ask you if you have anything you wish to add. Unless you are expecting this question, it may floor you. Worse, it may start you off on an extended, extemporaneous speech. The board is not usually seeking more information. The question is principally to offer you a last opportunity to present further qualifications or to indicate that you have nothing to add. So, if you feel that a significant qualification or characteristic has been overlooked, it is proper to point it out in a sentence or so. Do not compliment the board on the thoroughness of their examination – they have been sketchy, and you know it. If you wish, merely say, "No thank you, I have nothing further to add." This is a point where you can "talk yourself out" of a good impression or fail to present an important bit of information. Remember, *you close the interview yourself.*

The chairman will then say, "That is all, Mr. _____, thank you." Do not be startled; the interview is over, and quicker than you think. Thank him, gather your belongings and take your leave. Save your sigh of relief for the other side of the door.

How to put your best foot forward

Throughout this entire process, you may feel that the board individually and collectively is trying to pierce your defenses, seek out your hidden weaknesses and embarrass and confuse you. Actually, this is not true. They are obliged to make an appraisal of your qualifications for the job you are seeking, and they want to see you in your best light. Remember, they must interview all candidates and a non-cooperative candidate may become a failure in spite of their best efforts to bring out his qualifications. Here are 15 suggestions that will help you:

1) Be natural – Keep your attitude confident, not cocky

If you are not confident that you can do the job, do not expect the board to be. Do not apologize for your weaknesses, try to bring out your strong points. The board is interested in a positive, not negative, presentation. Cockiness will antagonize any board member and make him wonder if you are covering up a weakness by a false show of strength.

2) Get comfortable, but don't lounge or sprawl

Sit erectly but not stiffly. A careless posture may lead the board to conclude that you are careless in other things, or at least that you are not impressed by the importance of the occasion. Either conclusion is natural, even if incorrect. Do not fuss with your clothing, a pencil or an ashtray. Your hands may occasionally be useful to emphasize a point; do not let them become a point of distraction.

3) Do not wisecrack or make small talk

This is a serious situation, and your attitude should show that you consider it as such. Further, the time of the board is limited – they do not want to waste it, and neither should you.

4) Do not exaggerate your experience or abilities

In the first place, from information in the application or other interviews and sources, the board may know more about you than you think. Secondly, you probably will not get away with it. An experienced board is rather adept at spotting such a situation, so do not take the chance.

5) If you know a board member, do not make a point of it, yet do not hide it

Certainly you are not fooling him, and probably not the other members of the board. Do not try to take advantage of your acquaintanceship – it will probably do you little good.

6) Do not dominate the interview

Let the board do that. They will give you the clues – do not assume that you have to do all the talking. Realize that the board has a number of questions to ask you, and do not try to take up all the interview time by showing off your extensive knowledge of the answer to the first one.

7) Be attentive

You only have 20 minutes or so, and you should keep your attention at its sharpest throughout. When a member is addressing a problem or question to you, give him your undivided attention. Address your reply principally to him, but do not exclude the other board members.

8) Do not interrupt

A board member may be stating a problem for you to analyze. He will ask you a question when the time comes. Let him state the problem, and wait for the question.

9) Make sure you understand the question

Do not try to answer until you are sure what the question is. If it is not clear, restate it in your own words or ask the board member to clarify it for you. However, do not haggle about minor elements.

10) Reply promptly but not hastily

A common entry on oral board rating sheets is "candidate responded readily," or "candidate hesitated in replies." Respond as promptly and quickly as you can, but do not jump to a hasty, ill-considered answer.

11) Do not be peremptory in your answers

A brief answer is proper – but do not fire your answer back. That is a losing game from your point of view. The board member can probably ask questions much faster than you can answer them.

12) Do not try to create the answer you think the board member wants

He is interested in what kind of mind you have and how it works – not in playing games. Furthermore, he can usually spot this practice and will actually grade you down on it.

13) Do not switch sides in your reply merely to agree with a board member

Frequently, a member will take a contrary position merely to draw you out and to see if you are willing and able to defend your point of view. Do not start a debate, yet do not surrender a good position. If a position is worth taking, it is worth defending.

14) Do not be afraid to admit an error in judgment if you are shown to be wrong

The board knows that you are forced to reply without any opportunity for careful consideration. Your answer may be demonstrably wrong. If so, admit it and get on with the interview.

15) Do not dwell at length on your present job

The opening question may relate to your present assignment. Answer the question but do not go into an extended discussion. You are being examined for a *new* job, not your present one. As a matter of fact, try to phrase ALL your answers in terms of the job for which you are being examined.

Basis of Rating

Probably you will forget most of these "do's" and "don'ts" when you walk into the oral interview room. Even remembering them all will not ensure you a passing grade. Perhaps you did not have the qualifications in the first place. But remembering them will help you to put your best foot forward, without treading on the toes of the board members.

Rumor and popular opinion to the contrary notwithstanding, an oral board wants you to make the best appearance possible. They know you are under pressure – but they also want to see how you respond to it as a guide to what your reaction would be under the pressures of the job you seek. They will be influenced by the degree of poise you display, the personal traits you show and the manner in which you respond.

ABOUT THIS BOOK

This book contains tests divided into Examination Sections. Go through each test, answering every question in the margin. At the end of each test look at the answer key and check your answers. On the ones you got wrong, look at the right answer choice and learn. Do not fill in the answers first. Do not memorize the questions and answers, but understand the answer and principles involved. On your test, the questions will likely be different from the samples. Questions are changed and new ones added. If you understand these past questions you should have success with any changes that arise. Tests may consist of several types of questions. We have additional books on each subject should more study be advisable or necessary for you. Finally, the more you study, the better prepared you will be. This book is intended to be the last thing you study before you walk into the examination room. Prior study of relevant texts is also recommended. NLC publishes some of these in our Fundamental Series. Knowledge and good sense are important factors in passing your exam. Good luck also helps. So now study this Passbook, absorb the material contained within and take that knowledge into the examination. Then do your best to pass that exam.

———

EXAMINATION SECTION

Effectively Interacting with Agency Staff and Members of the Public

Test material will be presented in a multiple-choice question format.

Test Task: You will be presented with a variety of situations in which you must apply knowledge of how best to interact with other people.

SAMPLE QUESTION:

A person approaches you expressing anger about a recent action by your department. Which one of the following should be your first response to this person?

   A. Interrupt to say you cannot discuss the situation until he calms down.
   B. Say you are sorry that he has been negatively affected by your department's action.
   C. Listen and express understanding that he has been upset by your department's action.
   D. Give him an explanation of the reasons for your department's action.

The correct answer to this sample question is Choice C. *Solution:*

Choice A is not correct. It would be inappropriate to interrupt. In addition, saying that you cannot discuss the situation until the person calms down will likely aggravate the person further.

Choice B is not correct. Apologizing for your department's action implies that the action was improper.

Choice C is the correct answer to this question. By listening and expressing understanding that your department's action has upset the person, you demonstrate that you have heard and understand the person's feelings and point of view.

Choice D is not correct. While an explanation of the reasons for the action may be appropriate at a later time, at this moment the person is angry and would not be receptive to such an explanation.

EXAMINATION SECTION
TEST 1

DIRECTIONS: Each question or incomplete statement is followed by several suggested answers or completions. Select the one that BEST answers the question or completes the statement. *PRINT THE LETTER OF THE CORRECT ANSWER IN THE SPACE AT THE RIGHT.*

1. When conducting a needs assessment for the purpose of education planning, an agency's FIRST step is to identify or provide

    A. a profile of population characteristics
    B. barriers to participation
    C. existing resources
    D. profiles of competing resources

1.____

2. Research has demonstrated that of the following, the most effective medium for communicating with external publics is/are

    A. video news releases
    B. television
    C. radio
    D. newspapers

2.____

3. Basic ideas behind the effort to influence the attitudes and behaviors of a constituency include each of the following, EXCEPT the idea that

    A. words, rather than actions or events, are most likely to motivate
    B. demands for action are a usual response
    C. self-interest usually figures heavily into public involvement
    D. the reliability of change programs is difficult to assess

3.____

4. An agency representative is trying to craft a pithy message to constituents in order to encourage the use of agency program resources. Choosing an audience for such messages is easiest when the message

    A. is project- or behavior-based
    B. is combined with other messages
    C. is abstract
    D. has a broad appeal

4.____

5. Of the following factors, the most important to the success of an agency's external education or communication programs is the

    A. amount of resources used to implement them
    B. public's prior experiences with the agency
    C. real value of the program to the public
    D. commitment of the internal audience

5.____

6. A representative for a state agency is being interviewed by a reporter from a local news network. The representative is being asked to defend a program that is extremely unpopular in certain parts of the municipality. When a constituency is known to be opposed to a position, the most useful communication strategy is to present

6.____

A. only the arguments that are consistent with constituents' views
B. only the agency's side of the issue
C. both sides of the argument as clearly as possible
D. both sides of the argument, omitting key information about the opposing position

7. The most significant barriers to effective agency community relations include 7.____
      I.   widespread distrust of communication strategies
      II. the media's "watchdog" stance
      III. public apathy
      IV. statutory opposition

A. I only
B. I and II
C. II and III
D. III and IV

8. In conducting an education program, many agencies use workshops and seminars in a 8.____
classroom setting. Advantages of classroom-style teaching over other means of educating the public include each of the following, EXCEPT:

A. enabling an instructor to verify learning through testing and interaction with the target audience
B. enabling hands-on practice and other participatory learning techniques
C. ability to reach an unlimited number of participants in a given length of time
D. ability to convey the latest, most up-to-date information

9. The _____ model of community relations is characterized by an attempt to persuade 9.____
the public to adopt the agency's point of view.

A. two-way symmetric
B. two-way asymmetric
C. public information
D. press agency/publicity

10. Important elements of an internal situation analysis include the 10.____
      I.   list of agency opponents
      II. communication audit
      III. updated organizational almanac
      IV. stakeholder analysis

A. I and II
B. I, II and III
C. II and III
D. I, II, III and IV

11. Government agency information efforts typically involve each of the following objectives, 11.____
EXCEPT to

A. implement changes in the policies of government agencies to align with public opinion
B. communicate the work of agencies
C. explain agency techniques in a way that invites input from citizens
D. provide citizen feedback to government administrators

12. Factors that are likely to influence the effectiveness of an educational campaign include the

     I.   level of homogeneity among intended participants
     II.   number and types of media used
     III.   receptivity of the intended participants
     IV.   level of specificity in the message or behavior to be taught

    A.   I and II
    B.   I, II and III
    C.   II and III
    D.   I, II, III and IV

12.____

13. An agency representative is writing instructional objectives that will later help to measure the effectiveness of an educational program. Which of the following verbs, included in an objective, would be MOST helpful for the purpose of measuring effectiveness?

    A.   Know
    B.   Identify
    C.   Learn
    D.   Comprehend

13.____

14. A state education agency wants to encourage participation in a program that has just received a boost through new federal legislation. The program is intended to include participants from a wide variety of socioeconomic and other demographic characteristics. The agency wants to launch a broad-based program that will inform virtually every interested party in the state about the program's new circumstances. In attempting to deliver this message to such a wide-ranging constituency, the agency's best practice would be to

    A.   broadcast the same message through as many different media channels as possible
    B.   focus on one discrete segment of the public at a time
    C.   craft a message whose appeal is as broad as the public itself
    D.   let the program's achievements speak for themselves and rely on word-of-mouth

14.____

15. Advantages associated with using the World Wide Web as an educational tool include

     I.   an appeal to younger generations of the public
     II.   visually-oriented, interactive learning
     III.   learning that is not confined by space, time, or institutional association
     IV.   a variety of methods for verifying use and learning

    A.   I only
    B.   I and II
    C.   I, II and III
    D.   I, II, III and IV

15.____

16. In agencies involved in health care, community relations is a critical function because it

    A.   serves as an intermediary between the agency and consumers
    B.   generates a clear mission statement for agency goals and priorities
    C.   ensures patient privacy while satisfying the media's right to information
    D.   helps marketing professionals determine the wants and needs of agency constituents

16.____

17. After an extensive campaign to promote its newest program to constituents, an agency learns that most of the audience did not understand the intended message. Most likely, the agency has

    A. chosen words that were intended to inform, rather than persuade
    B. not accurately interpreted what the audience really needed to know
    C. overestimated the ability of the audience to receive and process the message
    D. compensated for noise that may have interrupted the message

17.____

18. The necessary elements that lead to conviction and motivation in the minds of participants in an educational or information program include each of the following, EXCEPT the _____ of the message.

    A. acceptability
    B. intensity
    C. single-channel appeal
    D. pervasiveness

18.____

19. Printed materials are often at the core of educational programs provided by public agencies. The primary disadvantage associated with print is that it

    A. does not enable comprehensive treatment of a topic
    B. is generally unreliable in term of assessing results
    C. is often the most expensive medium available
    D. is constrained by time

19.____

20. Traditional thinking on public opinion holds that there is about _____ percent of the public who are pivotal to shifting the balance and momentum of opinion—they are concerned about an issue, but not fanatical, and interested enough to pay attention to a reasoned discussion.

    A. 2
    B. 10
    C. 33
    D. 51

20.____

21. One of the most useful guidelines for influencing attitude change among people is to

    A. invite the target audience to come to you, rather than approaching them
    B. use moral appeals as the primary approach
    C. use concrete images to enable people to see the results of behaviors or indifference
    D. offer tangible rewards to people for changes in behaviors

21.____

22. An agency is attempting to evaluate the effectiveness of its educational program. For this purpose, it wants to observe several focus groups discussing the same program. Which of the following would NOT be a guideline for the use of focus groups?

    A. Focus groups should only include those who have participated in the program.
    B. Be sure to accurately record the discussion.
    C. The same questions should be asked at each focus group meeting.
    D. It is often helpful to have a neutral, non-agency employee facilitate discussions.

22.____

23. Research consistently shows that _____ is the determinant most likely to make a news-   23.____
paper editor run a news release.

    A. novelty
    B. prominence
    C. proximity
    D. conflict

24. Which of the following is NOT one of the major variables to take into account when con-   24.____
sidering a population-needs assessment?

    A. State of program development
    B. Resources available
    C. Demographics
    D. Community attitudes

25. The first step in any communications audit is to   25.____

    A. develop a research instrument
    B. determine how the organization currently communicates
    C. hire a contractor
    D. determine which audience to assess

————

KEY (CORRECT ANSWERS)

1.	A		11.	A
2.	D		12.	D
3.	A		13.	B
4.	A		14.	B
5.	D		15.	C
6.	C		16.	A
7.	D		17.	B
8.	C		18.	C
9.	B		19.	B
10.	C		20.	B

21.	C
22.	A
23.	C
24.	C
25.	D

————

TEST 2

DIRECTIONS: Each question or incomplete statement is followed by several suggested answers or completions. Select the one that BEST answers the question or completes the statement. *PRINT THE LETTER OF THE CORRECT ANSWER IN THE SPACE AT THE RIGHT.*

1. A public relations practitioner at an agency has just composed a press release highlighting a program's recent accomplishments and success stories. In pitching such releases to print outlets, the practitioner should

    I.   e-mail, mail, or send them by messenger
    II.   address them to "editor" or "news director"
    III.   have an assistant call all media contacts by telephone
    IV.   ask reporters or editors how they prefer to receive them

    A. I and II   B. I and IV   C. II, III and IV   D. III only

1.____

2. The "output goals" of an educational program are MOST likely to include

    A. specified ratings of services by participants on a standardized scale
    B. observable effects on a given community or clientele
    C. the number of instructional hours provided
    D. the number of participants served

2.____

3. An agency wants to evaluate satisfaction levels among program participants, and mails out questionnaires to everyone who has been enrolled in the last year. The primary problem associated with this method of evaluative research is that it

    A. poses a significant inconvenience for respondents
    B. is inordinately expensive
    C. does not allow for follow-up or clarification questions
    D. usually involves a low response rate

3.____

4. A communications audit is an important tool for measuring

    A. the depth of penetration of a particular message or program
    B. the cost of the organization's information campaigns
    C. how key audiences perceive an organization
    D. the commitment of internal stakeholders

4.____

5. The "ABC's" of written learning objectives include each of the following, EXCEPT

    A. Audience   B. Behavior   C. Conditions   D. Delineation

5.____

6. When attempting to change the behaviors of constituents, it is important to keep in mind that

    I.   most people are skeptical of communications that try to get them to change their behaviors
    II.   in most cases, a person selects the media to which he exposes himself
    III.   people tend to react defensively to messages or programs that rely on fear as a motivating factor
    IV.   programs should aim for the broadest appeal possible in order to include as many participants as possible

    A. I and II   B. I, II and III   C. II and III   D. I, II, III and IV

6.____

7. The "laws" of public opinion include the idea that it is 　　　　　　7.____

    A. useful for anticipating emergencies
    B. not sensitive to important events
    C. basically determined by self-interest
    D. sustainable through persistent appeals

8. Which of the following types of evaluations is used to measure public attitudes before   8.____
and after an information/educational program?

    A. retrieval study
    B. copy test
    C. quota sampling
    D. benchmark study

9. The primary source for internal communications is/are usually   9.____

    A. flow charts
    B. meetings
    C. voice mail
    D. printed publications

10. An agency representative is putting together informational materials–brochures and a   10.____
newsletter–outlining changes in one of the state's biggest benefits programs. In assembling print materials as a medium for delivering information to the public, the representative should keep in mind each of the following trends:

    I. For various reasons, the reading capabilities of the public are in general decline
    II. Without tables and graphs to help illustrate the changes, it is unlikely that the message will be delivered effectively
    III. Professionals and career-oriented people are highly receptive to information written in the form of a journal article or empirical study
    IV. People tend to be put off by print materials that use itemized and bulleted (•) lists.

    A. I and II   B. I, II and III   C. II and III   D. I, II, III and IV

11. Which of the following steps in a problem-oriented information campaign would typically   11.____
be implemented FIRST?

    A. Deciding on tactics
    B. Determining a communications strategy
    C. Evaluating the problem's impact
    D. Developing an organizational strategy

12. A common pitfall in conducting an educational program is to

    A. aim it at the wrong target audience
    B. overfund it
    C. leave it in the hands of people who are in the business of education, rather than those with expertise in the business of the organization
    D. ignore the possibility that some other organization is meeting the same educational need for the target audience

12._____

13. The key factors that affect the credibility of an agency's educational program include

    A. organization
    B. scope
    C. sophistication
    D. penetration

13._____

14. Research on public opinion consistently demonstrates that it is

    A. easy to move people toward a strong opinion on anything, as long as they are approached directly through their emotions
    B. easier to move people away from an opinion they currently hold than to have them form an opinion about something they have not previously cared about
    C. easy to move people toward a strong opinion on anything, as long as the message appeals to their reason and intellect
    D. difficult to move people toward a strong opinion on anything, no matter what the approach

14._____

15. In conducting an education program, many agencies use meetings and conferences to educate an audience about the organization and its programs. Advantages associated with this approach include
        I. a captive audience that is known to be interested in the topic
        II. ample opportunities for verifying learning
        III. cost-efficient meeting space
        IV. the ability to provide information on a wider variety of subjects

    A. I and II
    B. I, III and IV
    C. II and III
    D. I, II, III and IV

15._____

16. An agency is attempting to evaluate the effectiveness of its educational programs. For this purpose, it wants to observe several focus groups discussing particular programs. For this purpose, a focus group should never number more than _____ participants.

    A. 5   B. 10   C. 15   D. 20

16._____

17. A _____ speech is written so that several agency members can deliver it to different audiences with only minor variations.

    A. basic   B. printed   C. quota   D. pattern

17._____

18. Which of the following statements about public opinion is generally considered to be FALSE?

    18.____

    A. Opinion is primarily reactive rather than proactive.
    B. People have more opinions about goals than about the means by which to achieve them.
    C. Facts tend to shift opinion in the accepted direction when opinion is not solidly structured.
    D. Public opinion is based more on information than desire.

19. An agency is trying to promote its educational program. As a general rule, the agency should NOT assume that

    19.____

    A. people will only participate if they perceive an individual benefit
    B. promotions need to be aimed at small, discrete groups
    C. if the program is good, the audience will find out about it
    D. a variety of methods, including advertising, special events, and direct mail, should be considered

20. In planning a successful educational program, probably the first and most important question for an agency to ask is:

    20.____

    A. What will be the content of the program?
    B. Who will be served by the program?
    C. When is the best time to schedule the program?
    D. Why is the program necessary?

21. Media kits are LEAST likely to contain

    21.____

    A. fact sheets
    B. memoranda
    C. photographs with captions
    D. news releases

22. The use of pamphlets and booklets as media for communication with the public often involves the disadvantage that

    22.____

    A. the messages contained within them are frequently nonspecific
    B. it is difficult to measure their effectiveness in delivering the message
    C. there are few opportunities for people to refer to them
    D. color reproduction is poor

23. The most important prerequisite of a good educational program is an

    23.____

    A. abundance of resources to implement it
    B. individual staff unit formed for the purpose of program delivery
    C. accurate needs assessment
    D. uneducated constituency

24. After an education program has been delivered, an agency conducts a program evalua-   24.____
tion to determine whether its objectives have been met. General rules about how to conduct such an education program evaluation include each of the following, EXCEPT that it

    A. must be done immediately after the program has been implemented.
    B. should be simple and easy to use
    C. should be designed so that tabulation of responses can take place quickly and
        inexpensively
    D. should solicit mostly subjective, open-ended responses if the audience was large

25. Using electronic media such as television as means of educating the public is typically   25.____
recommended ONLY for agencies that
    I. have a fairly simple message to begin with
    II. want to reach the masses, rather than a targeted audience
    III. have substantial financial resources
    IV. accept that they will not be able to measure the results of the campaign with
        much precision

    A. I and II
    B. I, II and III
    C. II and IV
    D. I, II, III and IV

KEY (CORRECT ANSWERS)

1.	B		11.	C
2.	C		12.	D
3.	D		13.	A
4.	C		14.	D
5.	D		15.	B
6.	B		16.	B
7.	C		17.	D
8.	D		18.	D
9.	D		19.	C
10.	A		20.	D

21.	B
22.	B
23.	C
24.	D
25.	D

EXAMINATION SECTION
TEST 1

DIRECTIONS: Each question or incomplete statement is followed by several suggested answers or completions. Select the one that BEST answers the question or completes the statement. *PRINT THE LETTER OF THE CORRECT ANSWER IN THE SPACE AT THE RIGHT.*

1.   Public organizations *usually* share each of the following customer-service problems with private organizations EXCEPT

    A.   aversion to risk
    B.   staff-heaviness
    C.   provision of reverse incentives
    D.   control-apportionment functions

1.____

2.   A service representative demonstrates interpersonal skills by

    A.   identifying a customer's expectations
    B.   learning how to use a new office telephone system
    C.   studying a competitor's approach to service
    D.   anticipating how a customer will react to certain situations

2.____

3.   Of the following, _____ is NOT generally considered to be a common reason for flaws in an organization's customer focus.

    A.   commissioned employee compensation
    B.   full problem-solving authority for front-line personnel
    C.   inadequate hiring practices
    D.   specific, case-oriented policy and procedural statements

3.____

4.   According to MOST research, approximately _____ percent of dissatisfied customers will actually complain, or make their dissatisfaction with a product known to the organization.

    A.   5   B.   25   C.   50   D.   75

4.____

5.   Which of the following is an example of an expected benefit associated with a product or service?

    A.   Before buying a car, a customer believes she will not have to take the car in for repairs every few months.
    B.   A customer in a sporting goods store tells a sales-person exactly what kind of trolling motor will meet the requirements of the lakes the customer wanted to fish.
    C.   A supermarket shopper buys a loaf of bread, believing that the bread will remain fresh for a few days.
    D.   An airline passenger discovers that the meals served on board are good.

5.____

6. During a meeting with a service representative, a customer makes an apparently reason-   6.____
able request. However, the representative knows that satisfying the customer's request
will violate a rule that is part of the organization's policy. Although the representative feels
that an exception to the rule should be made in this case, she is not sure whether an
exception can or should be made.
The BEST course of action for the representative would be to

   A.   deny the request and apologize, explaining the company policy
   B.   rely on good judgment and allow the request
   C.   try to steer the customer toward a similar but clearly permissible request
   D.   contact a manager or more experienced peer to handle the request

7. While organizing an effective customer service department, it would be LEAST effective   7.____
to

   A.   create procedures for relaying reasons for complaints to other departments
   B.   set up a clear chain-of-command for handling specific customer complaints
   C.   continually monitor performance of front-line personnel
   D.   give front-line people full authority to resolve all customer dissatisfaction

8. Of the following, _____ is an example of *tangible* service.   8.____

   A.   an interior decorator telling his/her ideas to a potential client
   B.   a salesclerk giving a written cost estimate to a potential buyer
   C.   an automobile salesman telling a showroom customer about a car's performance
   D.   a stockbroker offering investment advice over the telephone

9. As a rule, a customer service representative who handles telephones should always   9.____
answer a call within no more than _____ ring(s).

   A.   1   B.   3   C.   5   D.   8

10. In order to be as useful as possible to an organization, feedback received from custom-   10.____
ers should NOT be

   A.   portrayed on a line graph or similar device
   B.   used to provide a general overview
   C.   focused on end-use customers
   D.   available upon demand

11. Of all the customers who switch to competing organizations, approximately _____ per-   11.____
cent do so because of poor service.

   A.   25   B.   40   C.   75   D.   95

12. When customers offer information that is incorrect in their complaints, a service repre-   12.____
sentative should do each of the following EXCEPT

   A.   assume that the customer is making an innocent mistake
   B.   look for opportunities to educate the customer
   C.   calmly state a reasonable argument that will correct the customer's mistake
   D.   believe the customer until he/she is able to find proof of his/her error

13. In order to insure that a customer feels comfortable in a face-to-face meeting, a service representative should   13.____

    A. avoid discussing controversial issues
    B. use personal terms such as *dear* or *friend*
    C. address the customer by his/her first name
    D. tell a few jokes

14. Customer satisfaction is MOST effectively measured in terms of   14.____

    A. cost   B. benefit
    C. convenience   D. value

15. Making a sale is NOT considered good service when   15.____

    A. there are no alternatives to the subject of the customer's complaint
    B. when the original product or service is outdated
    C. an add-n feature will forestall other problems
    D. the product or service the customer has been using is the wrong product

16. When dealing with an indecisive customer, the service representative should   16.____

    A. expand available possibilities
    B. offer a way out of unsatisfying decisions
    C. ask probing questions for understanding
    D. steer the customer toward one particular decision

17. Of the following, _____ would NOT be a source of direct organizational service promises.   17.____

    A. advertising materials
    B. published organizational policies
    C. contracts
    D. the customer's past experience with the organization

18. Generally, the only kind of organization that can validly circumvent the requirements of customer service is one that   18.____

    A. cannot afford to staff an entire service department
    B. relies solely on the sale of ten or fewer items per year
    C. has little or no competition
    D. serves clients that are separated from consumers

19. When using the problem-solving approach to solve the problem of an upset customer, the service representative should FIRST   19.____

    A. express respect for the customer
    B. identify the customer's expectations
    C. outline a solution or alternatives
    D. listen to understand the problem

20. During face-to-face meetings with strangers such as service personnel, most North Americans consider a comfortable proximity to be   20.____

    A. 6 inches - 1 foot   B. 8 inches - 1 1/2 feet
    C. 1 1/2-2 feet   D. 2-4 feet

21. When answering phone calls, a service representative should ALWAYS do each of the following EXCEPT

    A. state his/her name
    B. give the name of the organization or department
    C. ask probing questions
    D. offer assistance

21._____

22. If a customer appears to be emotionally neutral when lodging a complaint, it would be MOST appropriate for a service representative to demonstrate _____ in reaction to the complaint.

    A. urgency   B. empathy
    C. nonchalance   D. surprise

22._____

23. When soliciting customer feedback, standard practice is to limit the number of questions asked to APPROXIMATELY

    A. 3-5   B. 5-10   C. 10-20   D. 15-40

23._____

24. A customer has purchased an item from a company and has been told that the item will be delivered in two weeks. However, a customer service representative later dis-covers that deliveries are running about three days behind schedule.
The MOST appropriate course of action for the representa-tive would be to

    A. call the customer immediately, apologize for the delay, and await the customer's response
    B. call the customer a few days before delivery is due and explain that the delay is the fault of the delivery company
    C. immediately send out a *loaner* of the ordered item to the customer
    D. wait for the customer to note the delay and contact the organization

24._____

25. Most research shows that _____ % of what is communicated between people during face-to-face meetings is conveyed through words alone.

    A. 10   B. 30   C. 50   D. 80

25._____

KEY (CORRECT ANSWERS)

1.	D		11.	B
2.	D		12.	C
3.	B		13.	A
4.	A		14.	D
5.	B		15.	A
6.	D		16.	B
7.	B		17.	D
8.	B		18.	C
9.	B		19.	A
10.	B		20.	C

21.	C
22.	D
23.	B
24.	A
25.	A

———

TEST 2

DIRECTIONS: Each question or incomplete statement is followed by several suggested answers or completions. Select the one that BEST answers the question or completes the statement. *PRINT THE LETTER OF THE CORRECT ANSWER IN THE SPACE AT THE RIGHT.*

1. When working cooperatively to identify specific internal service targets, personnel typi-   1._____
    cally encounter each of the following obstacles EXCEPT

    A. rapidly-changing work environment
    B. philosphical differences about the nature of service
    C. specialized knowledge of certain personnel exceeds that of others
    D. a chain-of-command that isolates the end user

2. Which of the following is an example of an external customer relationship?   2._____

    A. Baggage clerks to travelers
    B. Catering staff to flight attendants
    C. Managers to ticketing agents
    D. Maintenance workers to ground crew

3. When a service representative puts a customer's complaint in writing, results will be pro-   3._____
    duced more quickly than if the representative had merely told someone.
    Which of the following is NOT generally considered to be a reason for this?

    A. The complaint can be more easily routed to parties capable of solving the problem.
    B. Management will understand the problem more clearly.
    C. The representative can more clearly see the main aspects of the complaint.
    D. The complaint and response will become a part of a public record.

4. A customer service representative creates a client file, which contains notes about what   4._____
    particular clients want, need, and expect.
    Which of the following basic areas of learning is the representative exercising?

    A. Interpersonal skills
    B. Product and service knowledge
    C. Customer knowledge
    D. Technical skills

5. A customer complains that a desired product, which is currently on sale, is needed in at   5._____
    least two weeks, but the company is out of stock and the product will not be available for
    another four weeks.
    Of the following, the BEST example of a service *recovery* on the part of a representa-
    tive would be to

    A. apologize for the company's, inability to serve the customer while expressing a
        wish to deal with the customer in the future
    B. attempt to steer the customer's interest toward an unrelated product
    C. offer a comparable model at the usual retail price
    D. offer a comparable model at the same sale price

6. Of the following, _____ is NOT generally considered to be a function of closed question-   6._____
   ing when dealing with a customer.

   A. understanding requests
   B. getting the customer to agree
   C. clarifying what has been said
   D. summarizing a conversation

7. When dealing with a customer who speaks with a heavy foreign accent, a service repre-   7._____
   sentative should NOT

   A. speak loudly
   B. speak slowly
   C. avoid humor or witticism
   D. repeat what has been said

8. If a customer service representative is aware that time will be a factor in the delivery of   8._____
   service to a customer, the representative should FIRST

   A. warn the customer that the organization is under time constraints
   B. suggest that the customer return another time
   C. ask the customer to suggest a service deadline
   D. tell the customer when service can reasonably be expected

9. In relation to a customer service representative's view of an organization, the customer's   9._____
   view of the company tends to be

   A. more negative   B. more objective
   C. broader in scope   D. less forgiving

10. When asked to define the factors that determine whether they will do business with an   10._____
    organization, most customers maintain that _____ is the MOST important.

    A. friendly employees   B. having their needs met
    C. convenience   D. product pricing

11. While a customer is stating her service requirements, a service representative should do   11._____
    each of the following EXCEPT

    A. ask questions about complex or unclear information
    B. formulate a response to the customer's remarks
    C. repeat critical information
    D. attempt to roughly outline the customer's main points

12. If a customer service representative must deal with other members of a service team in   12._____
    order to resolve a problem, the representative should avoid

    A. conveying every single detail of a problem to others
    B. suggesting deadlines for problem resolution
    C. offering opinions about the source of the problem
    D. explaining the specifics concerning the need for resolution

13. Of the following, the LAST step in the resolution of a service problem should be

    A. the offer of an apology for the problem
    B. asking probing questions to understand and confirm the nature of the problem
    C. listening to the customer's description of the problem
    D. determining and implementing a solution to the problem

13._____

14. _____ is a poor scheduling strategy for a customer service representative.

    A. Performing the easiest tasks first
    B. Varying work routines
    C. Setting deadlines that will allow some restful work periods
    D. Doing similar jobs at the same time

14._____

15. The MOST defensible reason for the avoidance of customer satisfaction guarantees is

    A. buyer remorse
    B. repeated customer contact
    C. high costs
    D. ability of buyers to take advantage of guarantees

15._____

16. A customer service representative demonstrates knowledge and courtesy to customers and is able to convey trust, competence, and confidence.
Of the following service factors, the representative is demonstrating

    A. assurance
    C. empathy
    B. responsiveness
    D. reliability

16._____

17. If a service representative is involved in sales, _____ is NOT one of the primary pieces of information he/she will need to supply the customer.

    A. cost of product or service
    B. how the product works
    C. how to repair the product
    D. available payment plans

17._____

18. A customer appears to be experiencing extreme feelings of anger and frustration when lodging a complaint. The MOST appropriate reaction for a service representative to demonstrate is

    A. urgency
    C. nonchalance
    B. empathy
    D. surprise

18._____

19. Of the following obstacles to customer service, _____ is NOT generally considered to be unique to public organizations.

    A. ambivalence toward clients
    B. limited competition
    C. a rule-based mission
    D. *clients* who are not really *customers*

19._____

20. MOST customers report that the most frustrating aspect of waiting in line for service is   20.____

    A. not knowing how long they will have to wait for service
    B. rudeness on the part of service representatives
    C. being expected to wait for service at all
    D. unfair prioritizing on the part of service representatives

21. Which of the following is an example of an *assumed benefit* associated with a product or   21.____
service?
A customer

    A. buys a sporty sedan and finds that its tight turning ratio makes it easy to park
    B. visits a fast-food restaurant because she is in a hurry to get dinner over with
    C. buys a videotape and believes it will not cause damage to her VCR
    D. tells a salesman that he wants to purchase a high-status automobile

22. On an average, for every complaint received by an organization, there are actually about   22.____
_____ customers who have legitimate problems.

    A. 3   B. 5   C. 15   D. 25

23. Once a customer problem is identified, each of the following should become a part of the   23.____
service recovery process EXCEPT

    A. apologizing
    B. an offer of compensation
    C. empathetic listening
    D. sympathy

24. As a rule, customers who telephone organizations should not be put on hold for any   24.____
longer than

    A. 10 seconds   B. 60 seconds
    C. 5 minutes   D. 10 minutes

25. The LEAST effective way to make customers feel as if they are a part of a service team   25.____
would be to ask them for

    A. information about similar products/services they have used
    B. opinions about how to solve problems
    C. personally contact the department that can best help them
    D. opinions about particular products and services

KEY (CORRECT ANSWERS)

1.	B	11.	B
2.	A	12.	C
3.	D	13.	A
4.	C	14.	A
5.	D	15.	B
6.	A	16.	A
7.	A	17.	C
8.	C	18.	B
9.	C	19.	B
10.	B	20.	A

21.	C
22.	D
23.	D
24.	B
25.	C

EXAMINATION SECTION
TEST 1

DIRECTIONS: Each question or incomplete statement is followed by several suggested answers or completions. Select the one that BEST answers the question or completes the statement. *PRINT THE LETTER OF THE CORRECT ANSWER IN THE SPACE AT THE RIGHT.*

1. In public agencies, communications should be based PRIMARILY on a

    A. two-way flow from the top down and from the bottom up, most of which should be given in writing to avoid ambiguity
    B. multidirection flow among all levels and with outside persons
    C. rapid, internal one-way flow from the top down
    D. two-way flow of information, most of which should be given orally for purposes of clarity

1.____

2. In some organizations, changes in policy or procedures are often communicated by word of mouth from supervisors to employees with no prior discussion or exchange of view-points with employees.
This procedure often produces employee dissatisfaction CHIEFLY because

    A. information is mostly unusable since a considerable amount of time is required to transmit information
    B. lower-level supervisors tend to be excessively concerned with minor details
    C. management has failed to seek employees' advice before making changes
    D. valuable staff time is lost between decision-making and the implementation of deci-sions

2.____

3. For good letter writing, you should try to visualize the person to whom you are writing, especially if you know him.
Of the following rules, it is LEAST helpful in such visualization to think of

    A. the person's likes and dislikes, his concerns, and his needs
    B. what you would be likely to say if speaking in person
    C. what you would expect to be asked if speaking in person
    D. your official position in order to be certain that your words are proper

3.____

4. One approach to good informal letter writing is to make letters sound conversational.
All of the following practices will usually help to do this EXCEPT:

    A. If possible, use a style which is similar to the style used when speaking
    B. Substitute phrases for single words (e.g., *at the present time* for *now*)
    C. Use contractions of words (e.g., *you're* for *you are*)
    D. Use ordinary vocabulary when possible

4.____

5. All of the following rules will aid in producing clarity in report-writing EXCEPT:

    A. Give specific details or examples, if possible
    B. Keep related words close together in each sentence
    C. Present information in sequential order
    D. Put several thoughts or ideas in each paragraph

5.____

6. The one of the following statements about public relations which is MOST accurate is that   6.____

    A. in the long run, appearance gains better results than performance
    B. objectivity is decreased if outside public relations consultants are employed
    C. public relations is the responsibility of every employee
    D. public relations should be based on a formal publicity program

7. The form of communication which is usually considered to be MOST personally directed to the intended recipient is the   7.____

    A. brochure   B. film   C. letter   D. radio

8. In general, a document that presents an organization's views or opinions on a particular topic is MOST accurately known as a   8.____

    A. tear sheet   B. position paper
    C. flyer   D. journal

9. Assume that you have been asked to speak before an organization of persons who oppose a newly announced program in which you are involved. You feel tense about talking to this group.
Which of the following rules generally would be MOST useful in gaining rapport when speaking before the audience?   9.____

    A. Impress them with your experience
    B. Stress all areas of disagreement
    C. Talk to the group as to one person
    D. Use formal grammar and language

10. An organization must have an effective public relations program since, at its best, public relations is a bridge to change.   10.____
All of the following statements about communication and human behavior have validity EXCEPT:

    A. People are more likely to talk about controversial matters with like-minded people than with those holding other views
    B. The earlier an experience, the more powerful its effect since it influences how later experiences will be interpreted
    C. In periods of social tension, official sources gain increased believability
    D. Those who are already interested in a topic are the ones who are most open to receive new communications about it

11. An employee should be encouraged to talk easily and frankly when he is dealing with his supervisor.   11.____
In order to encourage such free communication, it would be MOST appropriate for a supervisor to behave in a(n)

    A. sincere manner; assure the employee that you will deal with him honestly and openly
    B. official manner; you are a supervisor and must always act formally with subordinates

C. investigative manner; you must probe and question to get to a basis of trust
D. unemotional manner; the employee's emotions and background should play no part in your dealings with him

12. Research findings show that an increase in free communication within an agency GEN-ERALLY results in which one of the following?   12._____

A. Improved morale and productivity
B. Increased promotional opportunities
C. An increase in authority
D. A spirit of honesty

13. Assume that you are a supervisor and your superiors have given you a new-type procedure to be followed.   13._____
Before passing this information on to your subordinates, the one of the following actions that you should take FIRST is to

A. ask your superiors to send out a memorandum to the entire staff
B. clarify the procedure in your own mind
C. set up a training course to provide instruction on the new procedure
D. write a memorandum to your subordinates

14. Communication is necessary for an organization to be effective.   14._____
The one of the following which is LEAST important for most communication systems is that

A. messages are sent quickly and directly to the person who needs them to operate
B. information should be conveyed understandably and accurately
C. the method used to transmit information should be kept secret so that security can be maintained
D. senders of messages must know how their messages are received and acted upon

15. Which one of the following is the CHIEF advantage of listening willingly to subordinates and encouraging them to talk freely and honestly?   15._____
It

A. reveals to supervisors the degree to which ideas that are passed down are accepted by subordinates
B. reduces the participation of subordinates in the operation of the department
C. encourages subordinates to try for promotion
D. enables supervisors to learn more readily what the *grapevine* is saying

16. A supervisor may be informed through either oral or written reports.   16._____
Which one of the following is an ADVANTAGE of using oral reports?

A. There is no need for a formal record of the report.
B. An exact duplicate of the report is not easily transmitted to others.
C. A good oral report requires little time for preparation.
D. An oral report involves two-way communication between a subordinate and his supervisor.

17. Of the following, the MOST important reason why supervisors should communicate   17._____
effectively with the public is to

    A. improve the public's understanding of information that is important for them to
know
    B. establish a friendly relationship
    C. obtain information about the kinds of people who come to the agency
    D. convince the public that services are adequate

18. Supervisors should generally NOT use phrases like *too hard*, *too easy*, and *a lot* PRINCI-   18._____
PALLY because such phrases

    A. may be offensive to some minority groups
    B. are too informal
    C. mean different things to different people
    D. are difficult to remember

19. The ability to communicate clearly and concisely is an important element in effective   19._____
leadership.
Which of the following statements about oral and written communication is GENER-
ALLY true?

    A. Oral communication is more time-consuming.
    B. Written communication is more likely to be misinterpreted.
    C. Oral communication is useful only in emergencies.
    D. Written communication is useful mainly when giving information to fewer than
twenty people.

20. Rumors can often have harmful and disruptive effects on an organization.   20._____
Which one of the following is the BEST way to prevent rumors from becoming a problem?

    A. Refuse to act on rumors, thereby making them less believable.
    B. Increase the amount of information passed along by the *grapevine*.
    C. Distribute as much factual information as possible.
    D. Provide training in report writing.

21. Suppose that a subordinate asks you about a rumor he has heard. The rumor deals with   21._____
a subject which your superiors consider *confidential*.
Which of the following BEST describes how you should answer the subordinate?
Tell

    A. the subordinate that you don't make the rules and that he should speak to higher
ranking officials
    B. the subordinate that you will ask your superior for information
    C. him only that you cannot comment on the matter
    D. him the rumor is not true

22. Supervisors often find it difficult to *get their message across* when instructing newly   22._____
appointed employees in their various duties.
The MAIN reason for this is generally that the

A.   duties of the employees have increased
B.   supervisor is often so expert in his area that he fails to see it from the learner's point of view
C.   supervisor adapts his instruction to the slowest learner in the group
D.   new employees are younger, less concerned with job security and more interested in fringe benefits

23. Assume that you are discussing a job problem with an employee under your supervision. During the discussion, you see that the man's eyes are turning away from you and that he is not paying attention.
In order to get the man's attention, you should FIRST

    23._____

A.   ask him to look you in the eye
B.   talk to him about sports
C.   tell him he is being very rude
D.   change your tone of voice

24. As a supervisor, you may find it necessary to conduct meetings with your subordinates. Of the following, which would be MOST helpful in assuring that a meeting accomplishes the purpose for which it was called?

    24._____

A.   Give notice of the conclusions you would like to reach at the start of the meeting.
B.   Delay the start of the meeting until everyone is present.
C.   Write down points to be discussed in proper sequence.
D.   Make sure everyone is clear on whatever conclusions have been reached and on what must be done after the meeting.

25. Every supervisor will occasionally be called upon to deliver a reprimand to a subordinate. If done properly, this can greatly help an employee improve his performance.
Which one of the following is NOT a good practice to follow when giving a reprimand?

    25._____

A.   Maintain your composure and temper.
B.   Reprimand a subordinate in the presence of other employees so they can learn the same lesson.
C.   Try to understand why the employee was not able to perform satisfactorily.
D.   Let your knowledge of the man involved determine the exact nature of the reprimand.

KEY (CORRECT ANSWERS)

1.	C		11.	A
2.	B		12.	A
3.	D		13.	B
4.	B		14.	C
5.	D		15.	A
6.	C		16.	D
7.	C		17.	A
8.	B		18.	C
9.	C		19.	B
10.	C		20.	C

21.	B
22.	B
23.	D
24.	D
25.	B

———

TEST 2

DIRECTIONS: Each question or incomplete statement is followed by several suggested answers or completions. Select the one that BEST answers the question or completes the statement. *PRINT THE LETTER OF THE CORRECT ANSWER IN THE SPACE AT THE RIGHT.*

1. Usually one thinks of communication as a single step, essentially that of transmitting an idea.
   Actually, however, this is only part of a total process, the FIRST step of which should be

   A. the prompt dissemination of the idea to those who may be affected by it
   B. motivating those affected to take the required action
   C. clarifying the idea in one's own mind
   D. deciding to whom the idea is to be communicated

   1.____

2. Research studies on patterns of informal communication have concluded that most individuals in a group tend to be passive recipients of news, while a few make it their business to spread it around in an organization.
   With this conclusion in mind, it would be MOST correct for the supervisor to attempt to identify these few individuals and

   A. give them the complete facts on important matters in advance of others
   B. inform the other subordinates of the identify of these few individuals so that their influence may be minimized
   C. keep them straight on the facts on important matters
   D. warn them to cease passing along any information to others

   2.____

3. The one of the following which is the PRINCIPAL advantage of making an oral report is that it

   A. affords an immediate opportunity for two-way communication between the subordinate and superior
   B. is an easy method for the superior to use in transmitting information to others of equal rank
   C. saves the time of all concerned
   D. permits more precise pinpointing of praise or blame by means of follow-up questions by the superior

   3.____

4. An agency may sometimes undertake a public relations program of a defensive nature. With reference to the use of defensive public relations, it would be MOST correct to state that it

   A. is bound to be ineffective since defensive statements, even though supported by factual data, can never hope to even partly overcome the effects of prior unfavorable attacks
   B. proves that the agency has failed to establish good relationships with newspapers, radio stations, or other means of publicity
   C. shows that the upper echelons of the agency have failed to develop sound public relations procedures and techniques
   D. is sometimes required to aid morale by protecting the agency from unjustified criticism and misunderstanding of policies or procedures

   4.____

5. Of the following factors which contribute to possible undesirable public attitudes towards an agency, the one which is MOST susceptible to being changed by the efforts of the individual employee in an organization is that

    A. enforcement of unpopular regulations has offended many individuals
    B. the organization itself has an unsatisfactory reputation
    C. the public is not interested in agency matters
    D. there are many errors in judgment committed by individual subordinates

5.____

6. It is not enough for an agency's services to be of a high quality; attention must also be given to the acceptability of these services to the general public.
This statement is GENERALLY

    A. *false;* a superior quality of service automatically wins public support
    B. *true;* the agency cannot generally progress beyond the understanding and support of the public
    C. *false;* the acceptance by the public of agency services determines their quality
    D. *true;* the agency is generally unable to engage in any effective enforcement activity without public support

6.____

7. Sustained agency participation in a program sponsored by a community organization is MOST justified when

    A. the achievement of agency objectives in some area depends partly on the activity of this organization
    B. the community organization is attempting to widen the base of participation in all community affairs
    C. the agency is uncertain as to what the community wants
    D. there is an obvious lack of good leadership in a newly formed community organization

7.____

8. Of the following, the LEAST likely way in which a records system may serve a supervisor is in

    A. developing a sympathetic and cooperative public attitude toward the agency
    B. improving the quality of supervision by permitting a check on the accomplishment of subordinates
    C. permit a precise prediction of the exact incidences in specific categories for the following year
    D. helping to take the guesswork out of the distribution of the agency

8.____

9. Assuming that the *grapevine* in any organization is virtually indestructible, the one of the following which it is MOST important for management to understand is:

    A. What is being spread by means of the *grapevine* and the reason for spreading it
    B. What is being spread by means of the *grapevine* and how it is being spread
    C. Who is involved in spreading the information that is on the *grapevine*
    D. Why those who are involved in spreading the information are doing so

9.____

10. When the supervisor writes a report concerning an investigation to which he has been assigned, it should be LEAST intended to provide 10.____

    A. a permanent official record of relevant information gathered
    B. a summary of case findings limited to facts which tend to indicate the guilt of a suspect
    C. a statement of the facts on which higher authorities may base a corrective or disciplinary action
    D. other investigators with information so that they may continue with other phases of the investigation

11. In survey work, questionnaires rather than interviews are sometimes used.
The one of the following which is a DISADVANTAGE of the questionnaire method as compared with the interview is the 11.____

    A. difficulty of accurately interpreting the results
    B. problem of maintaining anonymity of the participant
    C. fact that it is relatively uneconomical
    D. requirement of special training for the distribution of questionnaires

12. In his contacts with the public, an employee should attempt to create a good climate of support for his agency. This statement is GENERALLY 12.____

    A. *false;* such attempts are clearly beyond the scope of his responsibility
    B. *true;* employees of an agency who come in contact with the public have the opportunity to affect public relations
    C. *false;* such activity should be restricted to supervisors trained in public relations techniques
    D. *true;* the future expansion of the agency depends to a great extent on continued public support of the agency

13. The repeated use by a supervisor of a call for volunteers to get a job done is objectionable MAINLY because it 13.____

    A. may create a feeling of animosity between the volunteers and the non-volunteers
    B. may indicate that the supervisor is avoiding responsibility for making assignments which will be most productive
    C. is an indication that the supervisor is not familiar with the individual capabilities of his men
    D. is unfair to men who, for valid reasons, do not, or cannot volunteer

14. Of the following statements concerning subordinates' expressions to a supervisor of their opinions and feelings concerning work situations, the one which is MOST correct is that 14.____

    A. by listening and responding to such expressions the supervisor encourages the development of complaints
    B. the lack of such expressions should indicate to the supervisor that there is a high level of job satisfaction
    C. the more the supervisor listens to and responds to such expressions, the more he demonstrates lack of supervisory ability
    D. by listening and responding to such expressions, the supervisor will enable many subordinates to understand and solve their own problems on the job

15. In attempting to motivate employees, rewards are considered preferable to punishment PRIMARILY because

    A. punishment seldom has any effect on human behavior
    B. punishment usually results in decreased production
    C. supervisors find it difficult to punish
    D. rewards are more likely to result in willing cooperation

15.____

16. In an attempt to combat the low morale in his organization, a high-level supervisor publicized an *open-door* policy to allow employees who wished to do so to come to him with their complaints.
Which of the following is LEAST likely to account for the fact that no employee came in with a complaint?

    A. Employees are generally reluctant to go over the heads of their immediate supervisors.
    B. The employees did not feel that management would help them.
    C. The low morale was not due to complaints associated with the job.
    D. The employees felt that they had more to lose than to gain.

16.____

17. It is MOST desirable to use written instructions rather than oral instructions for a particular job when

    A. a mistake on the job will not be serious
    B. the job can be completed in a short time
    C. there is no need to explain the job minutely
    D. the job involves many details

17.____

18. If you receive a telephone call regarding a matter which your office does not handle, you should FIRST

    A. give the caller the telephone number of the proper office so that he can dial again
    B. offer to transfer the caller to the proper office
    C. suggest that the caller re-dial since he probably dialed incorrectly
    D. tell the caller he has reached the wrong office and then hang up

18.____

19. When you answer the telephone, the MOST important reason for identifying yourself and your organization is to

    A. give the caller time to collect his or her thoughts
    B. impress the caller with your courtesy
    C. inform the caller that he or she has reached the right number
    D. set a business-like tone at the beginning of the conversation

19.____

20. As soon as you pick up the phone, a very angry caller begins immediately to complain about city agencies and *red tape*. He says that he has been shifted to two or three different offices. It turns out that he is seeking information which is not immediately available to you. You believe you know, however, where it can be found. Which of the following actions is the BEST one for you to take?

    A. To eliminate all confusion, suggest that the caller write the agency stating explicitly what he wants.
    B. Apologize by telling the caller how busy city agencies now are, but also tell him directly that you do not have the information he needs.

20.____

C. Ask for the caller's telephone number and assure him you will call back after you have checked further.
D. Give the caller the name and telephone number of the person who might be able to help, but explain that you are not positive he will get results.

21. Which of the following approaches usually provides the BEST communication in the objectives and values of a new program which is to be introduced? 21.____

    A. A general written description of the program by the program manager for review by those who share responsibility
    B. An effective verbal presentation by the program manager to those affected
    C. Development of the plan and operational approach in carrying out the program by the program manager assisted by his key subordinates
    D. Development of the plan by the program manager's supervisor

22. What is the BEST approach for introducing change? 22.____
    A

    A. combination of written and also verbal communication to all personnel affected by the change
    B. general bulletin to all personnel
    C. meeting pointing out all the values of the new approach
    D. written directive to key personnel

23. Of the following, committees are BEST used for 23.____

    A. advising the head of the organization
    B. improving functional work
    C. making executive decisions
    D. making specific planning decisions

24. An effective discussion leader is one who 24.____

    A. announces the problem and his preconceived solution at the start of the discussion
    B. guides and directs the discussion according to pre-arranged outline
    C. interrupts or corrects confused participants to save time
    D. permits anyone to say anything at anytime

25. The human relations movement in management theory is basically concerned with 25.____

    A. counteracting employee unrest
    B. eliminating the *time and motion* man
    C. interrelationships among individuals in organizations
    D. the psychology of the worker

KEY (CORRECT ANSWERS)

1.	C		11.	A
2.	C		12.	B
3.	A		13.	B
4.	D		14.	D
5.	D		15.	D
6.	B		16.	C
7.	A		17.	D
8.	C		18.	B
9.	A		19.	C
10.	B		20.	C

21.	C
22.	A
23.	A
24.	B
25.	C

———

EXAMINATION SECTION
TEST 1

DIRECTIONS: Each question or incomplete statement is followed by several suggested answers or completions. Select the one that BEST answers the question or completes the statement. *PRINT THE LETTER OF THE CORRECT ANSWER IN THE SPACE AT THE RIGHT.*

1. Good procedure in handling complaints from the public may be divided into the following four principal stages: 1.____

      I.   Investigation of the complaint
      II.   Receipt of the complaint
      III.   Assignment of responsibility for investigation and correction
      IV.   Notification of correction

The ORDER in which these stages ordinarily come is:

  A. III, II, I, IV   B. II, III, I, IV
  C. II, III, IV, I   D. II, IV, III, I

2. The department may expect the MOST severe public criticism if   2.____

  A. it asks for an increase in its annual budget
  B. it purchases new and costly street cleaning equipment
  C. sanitation officers and men are reclassified to higher salary grades
  D. there is delay in cleaning streets of snow

3. The MOST important function of public relations in the department should be to   3.____

  A. develop cooperation on the part of the public in keeping streets clean
  B. get stricter penalties enacted for health code violations
  C. recruit candidates for entrance positions who can be developed into supervisors
  D. train career personnel so that they can advance in the department

4. The one of the following which has MOST frequently elicited unfavorable public comment has been   4.____

  A. dirty sidewalks or streets
  B. dumping on lots
  C. failure to curb dogs
  D. overflowing garbage cans

5. It has been suggested that, as a public relations measure, sections hold *open house* for the public.
The MOST effective time for this would be   5.____

  A. during the summer when children are not in school and can accompany their parents
  B. during the winter when snow is likely to fall and the public can see snow removal preparations
  C. immediately after a heavy snow storm when department snow removal operations are in full progress
  D. when street sanitation is receiving general attention as during *Keep City Clean* week

6. When a public agency conducts a public relations program, it is MOST likely to find that each recipient of its message will

    A. disagree with the basic purpose of the message if the officials are not well known to him

    B. accept the message if it is presented by someone perceived as having a definite intention to persuade

    C. ignore the message unless it is presented in a literate and clever manner

    D. give greater attention to certain portions of the message as a result of his individual and cultural differences

6.____

7. Following are three statements about public relations and communications:

    I. A person who seeks to influence public opinion can speed up a trend

    II. Mass communications is the exposure of a mass audience to an idea

    III. All media are equally effective in reaching opinion leaders

Which of the following choices CORRECTLY classifies the above statements into those which are correct and those which are not?

    A. I and II are correct, but III is not

    B. II and III are correct, but I is not

    C. I and III are correct, but II is not

    D. III is correct, but I and II are not

7.____

8. Public relations experts say that MAXIMUM effect for a message results from

    A. concentrating in one medium

    B. ignoring mass media and concentrating on *opinion makers*

    C. presenting only those factors which support a given position

    D. using a combination of two or more of the available media

8.____

9. To assure credibility and avoid hostility, the public relations man MUST

    A. make certain his message is truthful, not evasive or exaggerated

    B. make sure his message contains some dire consequence if ignored

    C. repeat the message often enough so that it cannot be ignored

    D. try to reach as many people and groups as possible

9.____

10. The public relations man MUST be prepared to assume that members of his audience

    A. may have developed attitudes toward his proposals --favorable, neutral, or unfavorable

    B. will be immediately hostile

    C. will consider his proposals with an open mind

    D. will invariably need an introduction to his subject

10.____

11. The one of the following statements that is CORRECT is:

    A. When a stupid question is asked of you by the public, it should be disregarded

    B. If you insist on formality between you and the public, the public will not be able to ask stupid questions that cannot be answered

    C. The public should be treated courteously, regardless of how stupid their questions may be

    D. You should explain to the public how stupid their questions are

11.____

12. With regard to public relations, the MOST important item which should be emphasized in an employee training program is that

    A. each inspector is a public relations agent
    B. an inspector should give the public all the information it asks for
    C. it is better to make mistakes and give erroneous information than to tell the public that you do not know the correct answer to their problem
    D. public relations is so specialized a field that only persons specially trained in it should consider it

12.____

13. Members of the public frequently ask about departmental procedures.
Of the following, it is BEST to

    A. advise the public to put the question in writing so ,that he can get a proper formal reply
    B. refuse to answer because this is a confidential matter
    C. explain the procedure as briefly as possible
    D. attempt to avoid the issue by discussing other matters

13.____

14. The effectiveness of a public relations program in a public agency such as the authority is BEST indicated by the

    A. amount of mass media publicity favorable to the policies of the authority
    B. morale of those employees who directly serve the patrons of the authority
    C. public's understanding and support of the authority's program and policies
    D. number of complaints received by the authority from patrons using its facilities

14.____

15. In an attempt to improve public opinion about a certain idea, the BEST course of action for an agency to take would be to present the

    A. clearest statements of the idea even though the language is somewhat technical
    B. idea as the result of long-term studies
    C. idea in association with something familiar to most people
    D. idea as the viewpoint of the majority leaders

15.____

16. The fundamental factor in any agency's community relations program is

    A. an outline of the objectives
    B. relations with the media
    C. the everyday actions of the employees
    D. a well-planned supervisory program

16.____

17. The FUNDAMENTAL factor in the success of a community relations program is

    A. true commitment by the community
    B. true commitment by the administration
    C. a well-planned, systematic approach
    D. the actions of individuals in their contacts with the public

17.____

18. The statement below which is LEAST correct is:

    A. Because of selection standards, the supervisor frequently encounters problems resulting from subordinates' inability to express themselves in the language of the profession

18.____

B. Distortion of the meaning of a communication is usually brought about by a failure to use language that has a precise meaning to others
C. The term *filtering* is the distortion or dilution of content of a communication that occurs as information is passed from individual to individual
D. The complexity of the *communications net* will directly affect

19. Consider the following three statements that may or may not be CORRECT: 19._____
    I. In order to prevent the stifling of communications flow, supervisors should insist that employees use the formal communications network
    II. Two-way communications are faster and more accurate than one-way communications
    III. There is a direct correlation between the effectiveness of communications and the total setting in which they occur
    The choice below which MOST accurately describes the above statement is:

    A. All 3 are correct
    B. All 3 are incorrect
    C. More than one of the statements is correct
    D. Only one of the statements is correct

20. The statement below which is MOST inaccurate is: 20._____

    A. The supervisor's most important tool in learning whether or not he is communicating well is feedback
    B. Follow-up is essential if useful feedback is to be obtained
    C. Subordinates are entitled, as a matter of right, to explanations from management concerning the reasons for orders or directives
    D. A skilled supervisor is often able to use the grapevine to good advantage

21. *Since concurrence by those affected is not sought, this kind of communication can be   21._____
    issued with relative ease.* The kind of communication being referred to in this quotation is

    A. autocratic   B. democratic   C. directive   D. free-rein

22. The statement below which is LEAST correct is: 22._____

    A. Clarity is more important in oral communicating than in written since the readers of a written communication can read it over again
    B. Excessive use of abbreviations in written communications should be avoided
    C. Short sentences with simple words are preferred over complex sentences and difficult words in a written communication
    D. The *newspaper* style of writing ordinarily simplifies expression and facilitates understanding

23. Which one of the following is the MOST important factor for the department to consider in   23._____
    building a good public image?

    A. A good working relationship with the news media
    B. An efficient community relations program
    C. An efficient system for handling citizen complaints
    D. The proper maintenance of facilities and equipment
    E. The behavior of individuals in their contacts with the public

24. It has been said that the ability to communicate clearly and concisely is the MOST impor-   24.____
tant single skill of the supervisor.
Consider the following statements:
    I. The adage, *Actions speak louder than words,* has NO application in superior/
      subordinate communications since good communications are accomplished
      with words
    II. The environment in which a communication takes place will *rarely* determine
      its effect
    III. Words are symbolic representations which must be associated with past
      experience or else they are meaningless
The choice below which MOST accurately describes the above statements is:

  A. I, II and III are correct
  B. I and II are correct, but III is not
  C. I and III are correct, but II is not
  D. III is correct, but I and II are not
  E. I, II, and III are incorrect

25. According to expert opinion, the effectiveness of an organization is very dependent upon   25.____
good upward, downward, and lateral communications. Lateral communications are most
important to the activity of coordinating the efforts of organizational units. Before real
communication can take place at any level, barriers to communication must be recognized, understood, and removed. Consider the following three statements:
    I. The *principal* barrier to good communications is a failure to establish empa-
      thy between sender and receiver
    II. The difference in status or rank between the sender and receiver of a com-
      munication may be a communications barrier
    III. Communications are easier if they travel upward from subordinate to supe-
      rior
The choice below which MOST accurately describes the above statements is:

  A. I, II and III are incorrect
  B. I and II are incorrect
  C. I, II, and III are correct
  D. I and II are correct
  E. I and III are incorrect

KEY (CORRECT ANSWERS)

1.	B		11.	C
2.	D		12.	A
3.	A		13.	C
4.	A		14.	C
5.	D		15.	C
6.	D		16.	C
7.	A		17.	D
8.	D		18.	A
9.	A		19.	D
10.	A		20.	C

21.	A
22.	A
23.	E
24.	D
25.	E

―――――

EVALUATING CONCLUSIONS IN LIGHT OF KNOWN FACTS

An ability needed in many state jobs is the ability to decide if a conclusion is true, based on a set of facts. (These questions can also be called "Logic".) First read the facts (or premises) that are given, and then look at the conclusion. Assume the facts are true, and decide if the conclusion is:

1. Necessarily true.
2. Probably, but not necessarily true.
3. Indeterminable, cannot be determined.
4. Probably, but not necessarily false.
5. Necessarily false.

These five answer choices (above) are the same for each inference question.

1. FACTS: If the Commission approves the new proposal, the agency will move to a new location immediately. If the agency moves, five new supervisors will be appointed immediately. The Commission approved the new proposal.

   CONCLUSION: No new supervisors were appointed.

   1. Necessarily true.
   2. Probably, but not necessarily true.
   3. Indeterminable, cannot be determined.
   4. Probably, but not necessarily false.
   5. Necessarily false.

2. FACTS: If the director retires, John Jackson, the associate director, will not be transferred to another agency. Jackson will be promoted to director if he is not transferred. The director retired.

   CONCLUSION: Jackson will be promoted to director.

   1. Necessarily true.
   2. Probably, but not necessarily true.
   3. Indeterminable, cannot be determined.
   4. Probably, but not necessarily false.
   5. Necessarily false.

3. FACTS: If the maximum allowable income for food stamp recipients is increased, the number of food stamp recipients will increase. If the number of food stamp recipients increases, more funds must be allocated to the food stamp program, which will require a tax increase. Taxes cannot be raised without the approval of Congress. Congress probably will not approve a tax increase.

CONCLUSION: The maximum allowable income for food stamp recipients will increase.

    1. Necessarily true.
    2. Probably, but not necessarily true.
    3. Indeterminable, cannot be determined.
    4. Probably, but not necessarily false.
    5. Necessarily false.

4. FACTS: If prices are raised and sales remain constant, profits will increase. Prices were raised and sales levels will probably be maintained.

CONCLUSION: Profits will increase.

    1. Necessarily true.
    2. Probably, but not necessarily true.
    3. Indeterminable, cannot be determined.
    4. Probably, but not necessarily false.
    5. Necessarily false.

5. FACTS: Some employees in the personnel department are technicians. Most of the technicians working in the personnel department are test development specialists. Lisa Jones works in the personnel department.

CONCLUSION: Lisa Jones is a technician.

    1. Necessarily true.
    2. Probably, but not necessarily true.
    3. Indeterminable, cannot be determined.
    4. Probably, but not necessarily false.
    5. Necessarily false.

INFERENCE QUESTION ANSWERS AND EXPLANATIONS

1. The correct answer is number 5 (necessarily false). The new proposal was approved. According to the facts, approval means that the agency will move, and moving to a new location means that five new supervisors will be appointed.

2. The correct answer is number 1 (necessarily true). According to the facts, the director retired, which means that Jackson will not be transferred and, therefore, will be promoted to director.

3. The correct answer is number 4 (probably, but not necessarily false). Since Congress probably will not approve a tax increase, the maximum allowable income for food stamp recipients probably will not increase.

4. The correct answer is number 2 (probably, but not necessarily true). According to the facts, profits will increase if prices are raised and sales remain constant. It is known that prices were raised. Although sales level will probably be maintained, this is not certain.

5. The correct answer is number 3 (indeterminable, cannot be determined). The facts give no indication of the proportion of employees who are technicians. Therefore, no conclusion can be drawn with respect to the probability that any one employee is a technician.

LOGICAL REASONING
EVALUATING CONCLUSIONS IN LIGHT OF KNOWN FACTS

EXAMINATION SECTION
TEST 1
COMMENTARY

This section is designed to provide practice questions in evaluating conclusions when you are given specific data to work with.

We suggest you do the questions three at a time, consulting the answer key and then the solution section for any questions you may have missed. It's a good idea to try the questions again a week before the exam.

In the validity of conclusion type of question, you are first given a reading passage which describes a particular situation. The passage may be on any topic, as it is not your knowledge of the topic that is being tested, but your reasoning abilities. The passage is likely to detail several proposed courses of action and factors affecting these proposals. The reading passage is followed by a conclusion based on the facts in the passage, or a description of a decision taken regarding the situation. The conclusion is followed by a number of statements which have a possible connection to the conclusion. For each statement, you are to determine whether:

- A. The statement proves the conclusion.
- B. The statement supports the conclusion but does not prove it.
- C. The statement disproves the conclusion.
- D. The statement weakens the conclusion but does not disprove it.
- E. The statement has no relevance to the conclusion.

Remember that the conclusion after the passage is to be accepted as the outcome of what actually happened, and that you are being asked to evaluate the impact each statement would have had on the conclusion.

Questions 1-8 are based on the following paragraph.

In May of 1993, Mr. Bryan inherited a clothing store on Main Street in a small New England town. The store has specialized in selling quality men's and women's clothing since 1885. Business has been stable throughout the years, neither increasing nor decreasing. He has an opportunity to buy two adjacent stores which would enable him to add a wider range and style of clothing. In order to do this, he would have to borrow a substantial amount of money. He also risks losing the goodwill of his present clientele.

CONCLUSION: On November 7, 1993, Mr. Bryan tells the owner of the two adjacent stores that he has decided not to purchase them. He feels that it would be best to simply maintain his present marketing position, as there would not be enough new business to support an expansion.

- A. The statement proves the conclusion.
- B. The statement supports the conclusion but does not prove it.
- C. The statement disproves the conclusion.
- D. The statement weakens the conclusion.
- E. The statement is irrelevant to the conclusion.

1. A large new branch of the county's community college holds its first classes in September of 1993.

    1.____

2. The town's largest factory shuts down with no indication that it will reopen.

    2.____

3. The 1990 United States Census showed that the number of children per household dropped from 2.4 to 2.1 since the 1980 census.

    3.____

4. Mr. Bryan's brother tells him of a new clothing boutique specializing in casual women's clothing which is opening soon.

    4.____

5. Mr. Bryan's sister buys her baby several items for Christmas at Mr. Bryan's store.

    5.____

6. Mrs. McIntyre, the President of the Town Council, brings Mr. Bryan a home-baked pumpkin pie in honor of his store's 100th anniversary. They discuss the changes that have taken place in the town, and she comments on how his store has maintained the same look and feel over the years.

    6.____

7. In October of 1993, Mr. Bryan's aunt lends him $50,000.

    7.____

8. The Town Council has just announced that the town is eligible for funding from a federal project designed to encourage the location of new businesses in the central districts of cities and towns.

    8.____

Questions 9-18 are based on the following paragraph.

    A proposal has been put before the legislative body of a small European country to require air bags in all automobiles manufactured for domestic use in that country after 1999. The air bag, made of nylon or plastic, is designed to inflate automatically within a car at the impact of a collision, thus protecting front-seat occupants from being thrown forward. There has been much support of the measure from consumer groups, the insurance industry, key legislators, and the general public. The country's automobile manufacturers, who contend the new crash equipment would add up to $1,000 to car prices and provide no more protection than existing seat belts, are against the proposed legislation.

CONCLUSION: On April 21, 1994, the legislature passed legislation requiring air bags in all automobiles manufactured for domestic use in that country after 1999.

    A. The statement proves the conclusion.
    B. The statement supports the conclusion but does not prove it.
    C. The statement disproves the conclusion.
    D. The statement weakens the conclusion.
    E. The statement is irrelevant to the conclusion.

9. A study has shown that 59% of car occupants do not use seat belts.

    9.____

10. The country's Department of Transportation has estimated that the crash protection equipment would save up to 5,900 lives each year.

    10.____

11. On April 27, 1993, Augusta Raneoni was named head of an advisory committee to gather and analyze data on the costs, benefits, and feasibility of the proposed legislation on air bags in automobiles.

    11.____

12. Consumer groups and the insurance industry accuse the legislature of rejecting passage of the regulation for political reasons.

12.____

13. A study by the Committee on Imports and Exports projected that the sales of imported cars would rise dramatically in 1999 because imported cars do not have to include air bags, and can be sold more cheaply.

13.____

14. Research has shown that air bags, if produced on a large scale, would cost about $200 apiece, and would provide more reliable protection than any other type of seat belt.

14.____

15. Auto sales in 1991 have increased 3% over the previous year.

15.____

16. A Department of Transportation report in July of 2000 credits a drop in automobile deaths of 4,100 to the use of air bags.

16.____

17. In June of 1994, the lobbyist of the largest insurance company receives a bonus for her work on the passage of the air bag legislation.

17.____

18. In 2000, the stock in crash protection equipment has risen three-fold over the previous year.

18.____

Questions 19-25 are based on the following paragraph.

On a national television talk show, Joan Rivera, a famous comedienne, has recently insulted the physical appearances of a famous actress and the dead wife of an ex-President. There has been a flurry of controversy over her comments, and much discussion of the incident has appeared in the press. Most of the comments have been negative. It appears that this time she might have gone too far. There have been cancellations of two of her five scheduled performances in the two weeks since the show was televised, and Joan's been receiving a lot of negative mail. Because of the controversy, she has an interview with a national news magazine at the end of the week, and her press agent is strongly urging her to apologize publicly. She feels strongly that her comments were no worse than any other she has ever made, and that the whole incident will *blow over* soon. She respects her press agent's judgment, however, as his assessment of public sentiment tends to be very accurate.

CONCLUSION: Joan does not apologize publicly, and during the interview she challenges the actress to a weight-losing contest. For every pound the actress loses, Joan says she will donate $1 to the Cellulite Prevention League.

A. The statement proves the conclusion.
B. The statement supports the conclusion but does not prove it.
C. The statement disproves the conclusion.
D. The statement weakens the conclusion.
E. The statement is irrelevant to the conclusion.

19. Joan's mother, who she is very fond of, is very upset about Joan's comments.

19.____

20. Six months after the interview, Joan's income has doubled.

20.____

21. Joan's agent is pleased with the way Joan handles the interview.

21.____

22. Joan's sister has been appointed Treasurer of the Cellulite Prevention League. In her report, she states that Joan's $12 contribution is the only amount that has been donated to the League in its first six months.

22.____

23. The magazine receives many letters commending Joan for the courage it took for her to apologize publicly in the interview.

23.____

24. Immediately after the interview appears, another one of Joan's performances is cancelled.

24.____

25. Due to a printers strike, the article was not published until the following week.

25.____

Questions 26-30 are based on the following paragraph.

The law-making body of Country X must decide what to do about the issue of videotaping television shows for home use. There is currently no law against taping shows directly from the TV as long as the videotapes are not used for commercial purposes. The increasing popularity of pay TV and satellite systems, combined with the increasing number of homes that own video-cassette recorders, has caused a great deal of concern in some segments of the entertainment industry. Companies that own the rights to films, popular television shows, and sporting events feel that their copyright privileges are being violated, and they are seeking compensation or the banning of TV home video-taping. Legislation has been introduced to make it illegal to videotape television programs for home use. Separate proposed legislation is also pending that would continue to allow videotaping of TV shows for home use, but would place a tax of 10% on each videocassette that is purchased for home use. The income from that tax would then be proportionately distributed as royalties to those owning the rights to programs being aired. A weighted point system coupled with the averaging of several national viewing rating systems would be used to determine the royalties. There is a great deal of lobbying being done for both bills, as the manufacturers of videocassette recorders and videocassettes are against the passage of the bills.

CONCLUSION: The legislature of Country X rejects both bills by a wide margin.

    A. The statement proves the conclusion.
    B. The statement supports the conclusion but does not prove it.
    C. The statement disproves the conclusion.
    D. The statement weakens the conclusion.
    E. The statement is irrelevant to the conclusion.

26. Country X's Department of Taxation hires 500 new employees to handle the increased paperwork created by the new tax on videocassettes.

26.____

27. A study conducted by the country's most prestigious accounting firm shows that the cost of implementing the proposed new videocassette tax would be greater than the income expected from it.

27.____

28. It is estimated that 80% of all those working in the entertainment industry, excluding performers, own video-cassette recorders.   28._____

29. The head of Country X's law enforcement agency states that legislation banning the home taping of TV shows would be unenforceable.   29._____

30. Financial experts predict that unless a tax is placed on videocassettes, several large companies in the entertainment industry will have to file for bankruptcy.   30._____

Questions 31-38.

DIRECTIONS: The following questions 31 through 38 are variations on the type of question you just had. It is important that you read the question very carefully to determine exactly what is required.

31. In this question, select the choice that is most relevant to the conclusion.   31._____

    1. The Buffalo Bills football team is in second place in its division.
    2. The New England Patriots are in first place in the same division.
    3. There are two games left to play in the season, and the Bills will not play the Patriots again.
    4. The New England Patriots won ten games and lost four games, and the Buffalo Bills have won eight games and lost six games.

CONCLUSION: The Buffalo Bills win their division.

    A. The conclusion is proved by sentences 1-4.
    B. The conclusion is disproved by sentences 1-4.
    C. The facts are not sufficient to prove or disprove the conclusion.

32. In this question, select the choice that is most relevant to the conclusion.   32._____

    1. On the planet of Zeinon there are only two different eye colors and only two different hair colors.
    2. Half of those beings with purple hair have golden eyes.
    3. There are more inhabitants with purple hair than there are inhabitants with silver hair.
    4. One-third of those with silver hair have green eyes.

CONCLUSION: There are more golden-eyed beings on Zeinon than green-eyed ones.

    A. The conclusion is proved by sentences 1-4.
    B. The conclusion is disproved by sentences 1-4.
    C. The facts are not sufficient to prove or disprove the conclusion.

33. In this question, select the choice that is most relevant to the conclusion.   33._____
John and Kevin are leaving Amaranth to go to school in Bethany. They've decided to rent a small truck to move their possessions. Joe's Truck Rental charges $100 plus 30¢ a mile. National Movers charges $50 more but gives free mileage for the first 100 miles. After the first 100 miles, they charge 25¢ a mile.

49

CONCLUSION: John and Kevin rent their truck from National Movers because it is cheaper.

    A. The conclusion is proved by the facts in the above paragraph.
    B. The conclusion is disproved by the facts in the above paragraph.
    C. The facts are not sufficient to prove or disprove the conclusion.

34. For this question, select the choice that supports the information given in the passage.   34.____
    Municipalities in Country X are divided into villages, towns, and cities. A village has a population of 5,000 or less. The population of a town ranges from 5,001 to 15,000. In order to be incorporated as a city, the municipality must have a population over 15,000. If, after a village becomes a town, or a town becomes a city, the population drops below the minimum required (for example, the population of a city goes below 15,000), and stays below the minimum for more than ten years, it loses its current status, and drops to the next category. As soon as a municipality rises in population to the next category (village to town, for example), however, it is immediately reclassified to the next category.
    In the 1970 census, Plainfield had a population of 12,000. Between 1970 and 1980, Plainfield grew 10%, and between 1980 and 1990 Plainfield grew another 20%. The population of Springdale doubled from 1970 to 1980, and increased 25% from 1980 to 1990. The city of Smallville's population, 20,283, has not changed significantly in recent years. Granton had a population of 25,000 people in 1960, and has decreased 25% in each ten year period since then. Ellenville had a population of 4,283 in 1960, and grew 5% in each ten year period since 1960.
    In 1990,

    A. Plainfield, Smallville, and Granton are cities
    B. Smallville is a city, Granton is a town, and Ellenville is a village
    C. Springdale, Granton, and Ellenville are towns
    D. Plainfield and Smallville are cities, and Ellenville is a town

35. For this question, select the choice that is most relevant to the conclusion.   35.____
A study was done for a major food distributing firm to determine if there is any difference in the kind of caffeine containing products used by people of different ages. A sample of one thousand people between the ages of twenty and fifty were drawn from selected areas in the country. They were divided equally into three groups.
Those individuals who were 20-29 were designated Group A, those 30-39 were Group B, and those 40-50 were placed in Group C.
It was found that on the average, Group A drank 1.8 cups of coffee, Group B 3.1, and Group C 2.5 cups of coffee daily. Group A drank 2.1 cups of tea, Group B drank 1.2, and Group C drank 2.6 cups of tea daily. Group A drank 3.1 8-ounce glasses of cola, Group B drank 1.9, and Group C drank 1.5 glasses of cola daily.

CONCLUSION: According to the study, the average person in the 20-29 age group drinks less tea daily than the average person in the 40-50 age group, but drinks more coffee daily than the average person in the 30-39 age group drinks cola.

    A. The conclusion is proved by the facts in the above paragraph.
    B. The conclusion is disproved by the facts in the above paragraph.
    C. The facts are not sufficient to prove or disprove the conclusion.

36. For this question, select the choice that is most relevant to the conclusion.   36._____

    1. Mary is taller than Jane but shorter than Dale.
    2. Fred is taller than Mary but shorter than Steven.
    3. Dale is shorter than Steven but taller than Elizabeth.
    4. Elizabeth is taller than Mary but not as tall as Fred.

CONCLUSION: Dale is taller than Fred.

    A. The conclusion is proved by sentences 1-4.
    B. The conclusion is disproved by sentences 1-4.
    C. The facts are not sufficient to prove or disprove the conclusion.

37. For this question, select the choice that is most relevant to the conclusion.   37._____

    1. Main Street is between Spring Street and Glenn Blvd.
    2. Hawley Avenue is one block south of Spring Street and three blocks north of Main Street.
    3. Glenn Street is five blocks south of Elm and four blocks south of Main.
    4. All the streets mentioned are parallel to one another.

CONCLUSION: Elm Street is between Hawley Avenue and Glenn Blvd.

    A. The conclusion is proved by the facts in sentences 1-4.
    B. The conclusion is disproved by the facts in sentences 1-4.
    C. The facts are not sufficient to prove or disprove the conclusion.

38. For this question, select the choice that is most relevant to the conclusion.   38._____

    1. Train A leaves the town of Hampshire every day at 5:50 A.M. and arrives in New London at 6:42 A.M.
    2. Train A leaves New London at 7:00 A.M. and arrives in Kellogsville at 8:42 A.M.
    3. Train B leaves Kellogsville at 8:00 A.M. and arrives in Hampshire at 10:42 A.M.
    4. Due to the need for repairs, there is just one railroad track between New London and Hampshire.

CONCLUSION: It is impossible for Train A and Train B to follow these schedules without colliding.

    A. The conclusion is proved by the facts in the above paragraph.
    B. The conclusion is disproved by the facts in the above passage.
    C. The facts are not sufficient to prove or disprove the conclusion.

KEY (CORRECT ANSWERS)

1.	D	11.	C	21.	D	31.	C
2.	B	12.	C	22.	A	32.	A
3.	E	13.	D	23.	C	33.	C
4.	B	14.	B	24.	B	34.	B
5.	C	15.	E	25.	E	35.	B
6.	D	16.	B	26.	C	36.	C
7.	B	17.	A	27.	B	37.	A
8.	A	18.	B	28.	E	38.	B
9.	B	19.	D	29.	B		
10.	B	20.	E	30.	D		

———

SOLUTIONS TO QUESTIONS

1. The answer is D. This statement weakens the conclusion, but does not disprove it. If a new branch of the community college opened in September, it could possibly bring in new business for Mr. Bryant. Since it states in the conclusion that Mr. Bryant felt there would not be enough new business to support the additional stores, this would tend to disprove the conclusion. Choice C would not be correct because it's possible that he felt that the students would not have enough additional money to support his new venture, or would not be interested in his clothing styles. It's also possible that the majority of the students already live in the area, so that they wouldn't really be a new customer population. This type of question is tricky, and can initially be very confusing, so don't feel badly if you missed it. Most people need to practice with a few of these types of questions before they feel comfortable recognizing exactly what they're being asked to do.

2. The answer is B. It supports the conclusion because the closing of the factory would probably take money and customers out of the town, causing Mr. Bryant to lose some of his present business. It doesn't prove the conclusion, however, because we don't know how large the factory was. It's possible that only a small percentage of the population was employed there, or that they found other jobs.

3. The answer is E. The fact that the number of children per household dropped slightly nationwide from 1970 to 1980 is irrelevant. Statistics showing a drop nationwide doesn't mean that there was a drop in the number of children per household in Mr. Bryant's hometown. This is a tricky question, as choice B, supporting the conclusion but not proving it, may seem reasonable. If the number of children per household declined nationwide, then it may not seem unreasonable to feel that this would support Mr. Bryant's decision not to expand his business. However, we're preparing you for promotional exams, not "real life." One of the difficult things about taking exams is that sometimes you're forced to make a choice between two statements that both seem like they could be the possible answer. What you need to do in that case is choose the <u>best</u> choice. Becoming annoyed or frustrated with the question won't really help much. If there's a review of the exam, you can certainly appeal the question. There have been many cases where, after an appeal, two possible choices have been allowed as correct answers. We've included this question, however, to help you see what to do should you get a question like this. It's most important not to get rattled, and to select the <u>best</u> choice. In this case, the connection between the statistical information and Mr. Bryant's decision is pretty remote. If the question had said that the number of children in Mr. Bryant's <u>town</u> had decreased, then choice B would have been a more reasonable choice. It could also help in this situation to visualize the situation. Picture Mr. Bryant in his armchair reading that, nationwide, the average number of children per household has declined slightly. How likely would this be to influence his decision, especially since he sells men's and women's clothing? It would take a while for this decline in population to show up, and we're not even sure if it applies to Mr. Bryant's hometown. Don't feel badly if you missed this, it was tricky. The more of these you do, the more comfortable you'll feel.

4. The answer is B. If a new clothing boutique specializing in casual women's clothing were to open soon, this would lend support to Mr. Bryant's decision not to expand, but would not prove that he had actually made the decision not to expand. A new women's clothing boutique would most likely be in competition with his existing business, thus making any possible expansion a riskier venture. We can't be sure from this, however, that he didn't go ahead and expand his business despite the increased competition. Choice A, proves the conclusion, would only be the answer if we could be absolutely sure from the statement that Mr. Bryant had actually <u>not</u> expanded his business.

5. The answer is C. This statement disproves the conclusion. In order for his sister to buy several items for her baby at Mr. Bryant's store, he would have to have changed his business to include children's clothing.

6. The answer is A. It definitely proves the conclusion. The passage states that Mr. Bryant's store had been in business since 1885. A pie baked in honor of his store's 100th anniversary would have to be presented sometime in 1985. The conclusion states that he made his decision not to expand on November 7, 1983. If, more than a year later Mrs. MacIntyre comments that his store has maintained the same look and feel over the years, it could not have been expanded, or otherwise significantly changed.

7. The answer is D. If Mr. Bryant's aunt lent him $50,000 in October, this would tend to weaken the conclusion, which took place in November. Because it was stated that Mr. Bryant would need to borrow money in order to expand his business, it would be logical to assume that if he borrowed money he had decided to expand his business, weakening the conclusion. The reason C, disproves the conclusion, is not the correct answer is because we can't be sure Mr. Bryant didn't borrow the money for another reason.

8. The answer is B. If Mr. Bryant's town is eligible for federal funds to encourage the location of new businesses in the central district, this would tend to support his decision not to expand his business. Funds to encourage new business would increase the likelihood of there being additional competition for Mr. Bryant's store to contend with. Since we can't say for sure that there would be direct competition from a new business, however, choice A would be incorrect. Note that this is also a tricky question. You might have thought that the new funds weakened the conclusion because it would mean that Mr. Bryant could easily get the money he needed. Mr. Bryant is expanding his present business, not creating a <u>new</u> business. Therefore he is not eligible for the funding.

9. The answer is B. This is a very tricky question. It's stated that 59% of car occupants don't use seat belts. The legislature is considering the use of air bags because of safety issues. The advantage of air bags over seat belts is that they inflate upon impact, and don't require car occupants to do anything with them ahead of time. Since the population has strongly resisted using seat belts, the air bags could become even more important in saving lives. Since saving lives is the purpose of the proposed legislation, the information that a small percentage of people use seat belts could be helpful to the passage of the legislation. We can't be sure that this is reason enough for the legislature to vote for the legislation, however, so choice A is incorrect.

10. The answer is B, as the information that 5,900 lives could be saved would tend to support the conclusion. Saving that many lives through the use of air bags could be a very persuasive reason to vote for the legislation. Since we don't know for sure that it's enough of a compelling reason for the legislature to vote for the legislation, however, choice A could not be the answer.

11. The answer is C, disproves the conclusion. If the legislation had been passed as stated in the conclusion, there would be no reason to appoint someone head of an advisory committee six days later to analyze the "feasibility of the proposed legislation." The key word here is "proposed." If it has been proposed, it means it hasn't been passed. This contradicts the conclusion and therefore disproves it.

12. The answer is C, disproves the conclusion. If the legislation had passed, there would be no reason for supporters of the legislation to accuse the legislature of rejecting the legislation for political reasons. This question may have seemed so obvious that you might have thought there was a trick to it. Exams usually have a few obvious questions, which will trip you up if you begin reading too much into them.

13. The answer is D, as this would tend to disprove the conclusion. A projected dramatic rise in imported cars could be very harmful to the country's economy and could be a very good reason for some legislators to vote against the proposed legislation. It would be assuming too much to choose C, however, because we don't know if they actually did vote against it.

14. The answer is B. This information would tend to support the passage of the legislation. The estimate of the cost of the air bags is $800 less than the cost estimated by opponents, and it's stated that the protection would be more reliable than any other type of seat belt. Both of these would be good arguments in favor of passing the legislation. Since we don't know for sure, however, how persuasive they actually were, choice A would not be the correct choice.

15. The answer is E, as this is irrelevant information. It really doesn't matter whether auto sales in 1981 have increased slightly over the previous year. If the air bag legislation were to go into effect in 1984, that might make the information somehow more relevant. But the air bag legislation would not take effect until 1989, so the information is irrelevant, since it tells us nothing about the state of the auto industry then.

16. The answer is B, supports the conclusion. This is a tricky question. While at first it might seem to prove the conclusion, we can't be sure that the air bag legislation is responsible for the drop in automobile deaths. It's possible air bags came into popular use without the legislation, or with different legislation. There's no way we can be sure that it was the proposed legislation mandating the use of air bags that was responsible.

17. The answer is A. If, in June of 1984, the lobbyist received a bonus "for her work on the air bag legislation," we can be sure that the legislation passed. This proves the conclusion.

18. The answer is B. This is another tricky question. A three fold stock increase would strongly suggest that the legislation had been passed, but it's possible that factors other than the air bag legislation caused the increase. Note that the stock is in "crash protection equipment." Nowhere in the statement does it say air bags. Seat belts, motorcycle helmets, and collapsible bumpers are all crash protection equipment and could have contributed to the increase. This is just another reminder to read carefully because the questions are often designed to mislead you.

19. The answer is D. This would tend to weaken the conclusion because Marsha is very fond of her mother and she would not want to upset her unnecessarily. It does not prove it, however, because if Marsha strongly feels she is right, she probably wouldn't let her mother's opinion sway her. Choice E would also not be correct, because we cannot assume that Marsha's mother's opinion is of so little importance to her as to be considered irrelevant.

20. The answer is E. The statement is irrelevant. We are told that Marsha's income has doubled but we are not told why. The phrase "six months after the interview" can be misleading in that it leads us to assume that the increase and the interview are related. Her income could have doubled because she regained her popularity but it could also have come from stocks or some other business venture. Because we are not given any reason for her income doubling, it would be impossible to say whether or not this statement proves or disproves the conclusion. Choice E is the best choice of the five possible choices. One of the problems with promotional exams is that sometimes you need to select a choice you're not crazy about. In this case, "not having enough information to make a determination" would be the best choice. However, that's not an option, so you're forced to work with what you've got. On these exams it's sometimes like voting for President, you have to pick the "lesser of the two evils" or the least awful choice. In this case, the information is more irrelevant to the conclusion than it is anything else.

21. The answer is D, weakens the conclusion. We've been told that Marsha's agent feels that she should apologize. If he is pleased with her interview, then it would tend to weaken the conclusion but not disprove it. We can't be sure that he hasn't had a change of heart, or that there weren't other parts of the interview he liked so much that they outweighed her unwillingness to apologize.

22. The answer is A. The conclusion states that Marsha will donate $1 to the Cellulite Prevention League for every pound the actress loses. Marsha's sister's financial report on the League's activities directly supports and proves the conclusion.

23. The answer is C, disproves the conclusion. If the magazine receives many letters commending Marsha for her courage in apologizing, this directly contradicts the conclusion, which states that Marsha didn't apologize.

24. The answer is B. It was stated in the passage that two of Marsha's performances were cancelled after the controversy first occurred. The cancellation of another performance immediately after her interview was published would tend to support the conclusion that she refused to apologize. Because we can't be sure, however, that her performance wasn't cancelled for another reason, choice A would be incorrect.

25. The answer is E, as this information is irrelevant. Postponing the article an extra week does not affect Marsha's decision or the public's reaction to it.

26. The answer is C. If 500 new employees are hired to handle the "increased paperwork created by the new tax on videocassettes", this would directly contradict the conclusion, which states that the legislature defeated both bills. (They should all be this easy.)

27. The answer is B. The results of the study would support the conclusion. If implementing the legislation was going to be so costly, it is likely that the legislature would vote against it. Choice A is not the answer, however, because we can't be sure that the legislature didn't pass it anyway.

28. The answer is E. It's irrelevant to the conclusion that 80% of all those working in the entertainment industry own videocassette recorders. Sometimes if you're not sure about these, it can help a lot to try and visualize the situation. Why would someone voting on this legislation care about this fact? It doesn't seem to be the kind of information that would make any difference or impact upon the conclusion.

29. The answer is B. The head of the law enforcement agency's statement that the legislation would be unenforceable would support the conclusion. It's possible that many legislators would question why they should bother to pass legislation that would be impossible to enforce. Choice A would be incorrect however, because we can't be sure that the legislation wasn't passed in spite of his statement.

30. The answer is D. This would tend to weaken the conclusion because the prospect of several large companies going bankrupt would seem to be a good argument in favor of the legislation. The possible loss of jobs and businesses would be a good reason for some people to vote for the legislation. We can't be sure, however, that this would be a compelling enough reason to ensure passage of the legislation so choice C is incorrect.

This concludes our section on the "Validity of Conclusion" type of questions.

We hope these weren't too horrible for you. It's important to keep in mind exactly what you've been given and exactly what they want you to do with it. It's also necessary to remember that you may have to choose between two possible answers. In that case you must choose the one that seems the best. Sometimes you may think there is no good answer. You will probably be right but you can't let that upset you. Just choose the one you dislike the least.

We want to repeat that it is unlikely that this exact format will appear on the exam. The skills required to answer these questions, however, are the same as those you'll need for the exam so we suggest that you review this section before taking the actual exam.

31. The answer is C. This next set of questions requires you to "switch gears" slightly, and get used to different formats. In this type of question, you have to decide whether the conclusion is proved by the facts given, disproved by the facts given, or neither because not enough information has been provided. Fortunately, unlike the previous questions, you don't have to decide whether particular facts support or don't support the conclusion. This type of question is more straight forward, but the reasoning behind it is the same. We are told that the Bills have won two games less than the Patriots, and that the Patriots are in first place and the Bills are in second place. We are also told that there are two games left to play, and that they won't play each other again. The conclusion states that the Bills won the division. Is there anything in the four statements that would prove this? We have no idea what the outcome of the last two games of the season was. The

Bills and Patriots could have ended up tied at the end of the season, or the Bills could have lost both or one of their last games while the Patriots did the same. There might even be another team tied for first or second place with the Bills or Patriots. Since we don't know for sure, Choice A is incorrect. Choice B is trickier. It might seem at first glance that the best the Bills could do would be to tie the Patriots if the Patriots lost their last two games and the Bills won their last two games. But it would be too much to assume that there is no procedure for a tiebreaker that wouldn't give the Bills the division championship. Since we don't know what the rules are in the event of a tie (for example, what if a tie was decided on the results of what happened when the two teams had played each other, or on the best record in the division, or on most points scored?), we can't say for sure that it would be impossible for the Bills to win their division. For this reason, choice C is the answer, as we don't have enough information to prove or disprove the conclusion. This question looked more difficult than it actually was. It's important to disregard any factors outside of the actual question, and to focus only on what you've been given. In this case, as on all of these types of questions, what you know or don't know about a subject is actually irrelevant. It's best to concentrate only on the actual facts given.

32. The answer is A. The conclusion is proved by the facts given.

In this type of problem it is usually best to pull as many facts as possible from the sentences and then put them into a simpler form. The phrasing and the order of exam questions are designed to be confusing so you need to restate things as clearly as possible by eliminating the extras.

Sentence 1 tells us that there are only two possible colors for eyes and two for hair. Looking at the other sentences we learn that eyes are either green or gold and that hair is either silver or purple. If half the beings with purple hair have golden eyes then the other half must have green eyes since it is the only other eye color. Likewise, if one-third of those with silver hair have green eyes the other two-thirds must have golden eyes.

This information makes it clear that there are more golden-eyed beings on Zeinon than green-eyed ones. It doesn't matter that we don't know exactly how many are actually living on the planet. The number of those with gold eyes (1/2 plus 2/3) will always be greater than the number of those with green eyes (1/2 plus 1/3), no matter what the actual figures might be. Sentence 3 is totally irrelevant because even if there were more silver-haired inhabitants it would not affect the conclusion.

33. The answer is C. The conclusion is neither proved nor disproved by the facts because we don't know how many miles Bethany is from Amoranth.

With this type of question, if you're not sure how to approach it you can always substitute in a range of "real numbers" to see what the result would be. If they were 200 miles apart Joe's Truck Rental would be cheaper because they would charge a total of $160 while National Movers would charge $175.

Joe's - $100 plus .30 x 200 (or $60) = $160
National - $150 plus .25 x 100 (or $25) = $175

If the towns were 600 miles apart, however, National Movers would be cheaper. The cost of renting from National would be $275 compared to the $280 charged by Joe's Trucking.

Joe's - $100 plus .30 x 600 (or $180) = $280
National - $150 plus .25 x 500 (or $125) = $275

34. The answer is B. We've varied the format once more, but the reasoning is similar. This is a tedious question that is more like a math question, but we wanted to give you some practice with this type, just in case. You won't be able to do this question if you've forgotten how to do percents. Many exams require this knowledge, so if you feel you need a review we suggest you read Booklets 1, 2 or 3 in this series.

The only way to attack this problem is to go through each choice until you find the one that is correct. Choice A states that Plainfield, Smallville and Granton are cities. Let's begin with Plainfield. The passage states that in 1960 Plainfield had a population of 12,000, and that it grew 10% between 1960 and 1970, and another 20% between 1970 and 1980. Ten percent of 12,000 is 1200 (12,000 x .10 = 1200). Therefore, the population grew from 12,000 in 1960 to 12,000 + 1200 between 1960 and 1970. At the time of the 1970 Census, Plainfield's population was 13,200. It then grew another 20% between 1970 and 1980, so, 13,200 x .20 = 2640. 13,200 plus the additional increase of 2640 would make the population of Plainfield 15,840. This would qualify it as a city, since its population is over 15,000. Since a change upward in the population of a municipality is re-classified immediately, Plainfield would have become a city right away. So far, statement A is true. The passage states that Smallville's population has not changed significantly in the last twenty years. Since Smallville's population was 20,283, Smallville would still be a city. Granton had a population of 25,000 (what a coincidence that so many of these places have such nice, even numbers) in 1950. The population has decreased 25% in each ten year period since that time. So from 1950 to 1960 the population decreased 25%. 25,000 x .25 = 6,250. 25,000 minus 6,250 = 18,750. So the population of Granton in 1960 would have been 18,750. (Or you could have saved a step and multiplied 25,000 by .75 to get 18,750.) The population from 1960 to 1970 decreased an additional 25%. So: 18,750 x .25 = 4687.50. 18,750 minus 4687.50 = 14,062.50. Or: 18,750 x .75 = 14,062.50. (Don't let the fact that a half of a person is involved confuse you, these are exam questions, not real life.) From 1970 to 1980 the population decreased an additional 25%. This would mean that Granton's population was below 15,000 for more than ten years, so it's status as a city would have changed to that of a town, which would make choice A incorrect, since it states that Granton is a city.

Choice B states that Smallville is a city and Granton is a town which we know to be true from the information above. Choice B is correct so far. We next need to determine if Ellenville is a village. Ellenville had a population of 4,283 in 1950, and increased 5% in each ten year period since 1950. 4,283 x .05 = 214.15. 4,283 plus 214.15 = 4,497.15, so Ellenville's population from 1950 to 1960 increased to 4,497.15. (Or: 4,283 x 1.05 - 4,497.15.) From 1960 to 1970 Ellenville's population increased another 5%: 4,497.15 x .05 = 224.86. 4,497.15 plus 224.86 = 4,772.01 (or: 4,497.15 x 1.05 = 4,722.01.) From 1970 to 1980, Ellenville's population increased another 5%: 4,722.01 x .05 = 236.1. 4722.01 plus 236.10 = 4958.11. (Or: 4,722.01 x 1.05 = 4958.11.).

Ellenville's population is still under 5,000 in 1980 so it would continue to be classified as a village. Since all three statements in choice B are true, Choice B must be the answer. However, we'll go through the other choices. Choice C states that Springdale is a town. The passage tells us that the population of Springdale doubled from 1960 to 1970, and increased

25% from 1970 to 1980. It doesn't give us any actual population figures, however, so it's impossible to know what the population of Springdale is, making Choice C incorrect. Choice C also states that Granton is a town, which is true, and that Ellenville is a town, which is false (from Choice B we know it's a village). Choice D states that Plainfield and Smallville are cities, which is information we already know is true, and that Ellenville is a town. Since Ellenville is a village, Choice D is also incorrect.

This was a lot of work for just one question and we doubt you'll get one like this on this section of the exam, but we included it just in case. On an exam, you can always put a check mark next to a question like this and come back to it later, if you feel you're pressed for time and could spend your time more productively on other, less time consuming problems.

35. The answer is B. This question requires very careful reading. It's best to break the conclusion down into smaller parts in order to solve the problem. The first half of the conclusion states that the average person in the 20-29 age group (Group A) drinks less tea daily than the average person in the 40-50 age group (Group C). The average person in Group A drinks 2.1 cups of tea daily, while the average person in Group C drinks 2.6 cups of tea daily. Since 2.1 is less than 2.6, the conclusion is correct so far. The second half of the conclusion states that the average person in Group A drinks more coffee daily than the average person in the 30-39 age group (Group B) drinks cola. The average person in Group A drinks 1.8 cups of coffee daily while the average person in Group B drinks 1.9 glasses of cola. This disproves the conclusion, which states that the average person in Group A drinks more coffee daily than the average person in Group B drinks cola.

36. The answer is C. The easiest way to approach a problem that deals with the relationship between a number of different people or things is to set up a diagram. This type of problem is usually too confusing to do in your head. For this particular problem the "diagram" could be a line, one end of which would be labelled tall and the other end labelled short. Then, taking one sentence at a time, place the people on the line to see where they fall in relation to one another.

The diagram of the first sentence would look like this:

Tall
(left)   Dale   Mary   Jane   Short
                                                    (right)

Mary is taller than Jane but shorter than Dale so she would fall somewhere between the two of them. We have placed tall on the left and labelled it left just to make the explanation easier. You could just as easily have reversed the position.

The second sentence places Fred somewhere to the left of Mary because he is taller than she is. Steven would be to the left of Fred for the same reason. At this point we don't know whether Steven and Fred are taller or shorter than Dale. The new diagram would look like this:

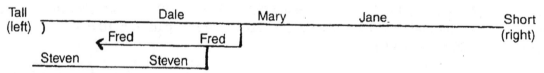

The third stentence introduces Elizabeth, presenting a new problem. Elizabeth can be anywhere to the right of Dale. Don't make the mistake of assuming she falls between Dale and Mary. At this point we don't know where she fits in relation to Mary, Jane, or even Fred.

We do get information about Steven, however. He is taller than Dale so he would be to the left of Dale. Since he is also taller than Fred (see sentence two) we know that Steven is the tallest person thus far. The diagram would now look like this:

| Tall (left) | | Dale | | Mary | Jane. | | Short (right) |

Fred ← Fred
Steven Steven

Fred's height is somewhere between Steven and Mary, Elizabeth's anywhere between Dale and the end of the line.

The fourth sentence tells us where Elizabeth stands, in relation to Fred and the others in the problem. The fact that she is taller than Mary means she is also taller than Jane. The final diagram would look like this:

| Tall (left) | Steven | Dale | Elizabeth | Mary | Jane | Short (right) |

Fred

We still don't know whether Dale or Fred is taller, however. Therefore, the conclusion that Dale is taller than Fred can't be proved. It also can't be disproved because we don't know for sure that he isn't. The answer has to be Choice C, as the conclusion can't be proved or disproved.

37. The answer is A. This is another problem that is easiest for most people if they make a diagram. Sentence 1 states that Main Street is between Spring Street and Glenn Blvd. At this point we don't know if they are next to each other or if they are separated by a number of streets. Therefore, you should leave space between streets as you plot your first diagram.

The order of the streets could go either:

Spring St.	or	Glenn Blvd.
Main St.		Main St.
Glenn Blvd.		Spring St.

Sentence 2 states that Hawley Street is one block south of Spring Street and 3 blocks north of Main Street. Because most people think in terms of north as above and south as below and because it was stated that Hawley is one block south of Spring Street and three blocks north of Main Street, the next diagram could look like this:

Spring
Hawley

———

———
Main
Glenn

The third sentence states that Glenn Street is five blocks south of Elm and four blocks south of Main. It could look like this:

Spring
Hawley

Elm
Main

Glenn

The conclusion states that Elm Street is between Hawley Avenue and Glenn Blvd. From the above diagram we can see that this is the case.

38. The answer is B. For most people the best way to do this problem is to draw a diagram, plotting the course of both trains. Sentence 1 states that train A leaves Hampshire at 5:50 a.m. and reaches New London at 6:42. Your first diagram might look like this:

38._____

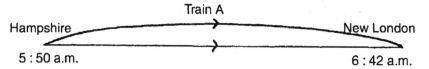

Sentence 2 states that the train leaves New London at 7:00 a.m. and arrives in Kellogsville at 8:42 a.m. The diagram might now look like this:

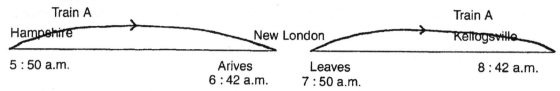

Sentence 3 gives us the rest of the information that must be included in the diagram. It introduces Train B, which moves in the opposite direction, leaving Kellogsville at 8:00 a.m. and arriving at Hampshire at 10:42 a.m. The final diagram might look like this:

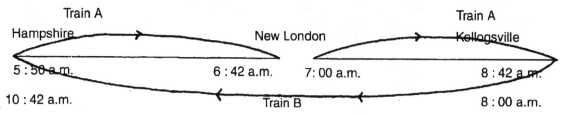

As you can see from the diagram, the routes of the two trains will overlap somewhere between Kellogsville and New London. If you read sentence 4 quickly and assumed that that was the section with only one track, you probably would have assumed that there would have had to be a collision. Sentence 4 states, however, that there is only one rail-road track between New London and Hampshire. That is the only section, then, where the two trains could collide. By the time Train B gets to that section, however, Train A will have passed it. The two trains will pass each other somewhere between New London and Kellogsville, not New London and Hampshire.

Evaluating Conclusions in Light of Known Facts

EXAMINATION SECTION
TEST 1

DIRECTIONS: Each question or incomplete statement is followed by several suggested answers or completions. Select the one that BEST answers the question or completes the statement. *PRINT THE LETTER OF THE CORRECT ANSWER IN THE SPACE AT THE RIGHT.*

Questions 1-9.

DIRECTIONS: In questions 1-9, you will read a set of facts and a conclusion drawn from them. The conclusion may be valid or invalid, based on the facts—it's your task to determine the validity of the conclusion.

For each question, select the letter before the statement that BEST expresses the relationship between the given facts and the conclusion that has been drawn from them. Your choices are:
A. The facts prove the conclusion
B. The facts disprove the conclusion; or
C. The facts neither prove nor disprove the conclusion.

1. FACTS: If the supervisor retires, James, the assistant supervisor, will not be transferred to another department. James will be promoted to supervisor if he is not transferred. The supervisor retired.

    CONCLUSION: James will be promoted to supervisor.

    A. The facts prove the conclusion.
    B. The facts disprove the conclusion.
    C. The facts neither prove nor disprove the conclusion.

1.____

2. FACTS: In the town of Luray, every player on the softball team works at Luray National Bank. In addition, every player on the Luray softball team wears glasses.

    CONCLUSION: At least some of the people who work at Luray National Bank wear glasses.

    A. The facts prove the conclusion.
    B. The facts disprove the conclusion.
    C. The facts neither prove nor disprove the conclusion.

2.____

3. FACTS: The only time Henry and June go out to dinner is on an evening when they have childbirth classes. Their childbirth classes meet on Tuesdays and Thursdays.

    CONCLUSION: Henry and June never go out to dinner on Friday or Saturday.

    A. The facts prove the conclusion.
    B. The facts disprove the conclusion.
    C. The facts neither prove nor disprove the conclusion.

3.____

4. FACTS: Every player on the field hockey team has at least one bruise. Everyone on the field hockey team also has scarred knees.

   CONCLUSION: Most people with both bruises and scarred knees are field hockey players.

   A. The facts prove the conclusion.
   B. The facts disprove the conclusion.
   C. The facts neither prove nor disprove the conclusion.

   4.____

5. FACTS: In the chess tournament, Lance will win his match against Jane if Jane wins her match against Mathias. If Lance wins his match against Jane, Christine will not win her match against Jane.

   CONCLUSION: Christine will not win her match against Jane if Jane wins her match against Mathias.

   A. The facts prove the conclusion.
   B. The facts disprove the conclusion.
   C. The facts neither prove nor disprove the conclusion.

   5.____

6. FACTS: No green lights on the machine are indicators for the belt drive status. Not all of the lights on the machine's upper panel are green. Some lights on the machine's lower panel are green.

   CONCLUSION: The green lights on the machine's lower panel may be indicators for the belt drive status.

   A. The facts prove the conclusion.
   B. The facts disprove the conclusion.
   C. The facts neither prove nor disprove the conclusion.

   6.____

7. FACTS: At a small, one-room country school, there are eight students: Amy, Ben, Carla, Dan, Elliot, Francine, Greg, and Hannah. Each student is in either the 6th, 7th, or 8th grade. Either two or three students are in each grade. Amy, Dan, and Francine are all in different grades. Ben and Elliot are both in the 7th grade. Hannah and Carl are in the same grade.

   CONCLUSION: Exactly three students are in the 7th grade.

   A. The facts prove the conclusion.
   B. The facts disprove the conclusion.
   C. The facts neither prove nor disprove the conclusion.

   7.____

8. FACTS: Two married couples are having lunch together. Two of the four people are German and two are Russian, but in each couple the nationality of a spouse is not necessarily the same as the other's. One person in the group is a teacher, the other a lawyer, one an engineer, and the other a writer. The teacher is a Russian man. The writer is Russian, and her husband is an engineer. One of the people, Mr. Stern, is German.

   CONCLUSION: Mr. Stern's wife is a writer.

   8.____

A. The facts prove the conclusion.
B. The facts disprove the conclusion.
C. The facts neither prove nor disprove the conclusion.

9. FACTS: The flume ride at the county fair is open only to children who are at least 36 inches tall. Lisa is 30 inches tall. John is shorter than Henry, but more than 10 inches taller than Lisa.

9.____

CONCLUSION: Lisa is the only one who can't ride the flume ride.

A. The facts prove the conclusion.
B. The facts disprove the conclusion.
C. The facts neither prove nor disprove the conclusion.

Questions 10-17.

DIRECTIONS: Questions 10-17 are based on the following reading passage. It is not your knowledge of the particular topic that is being tested, but your ability to reason based on what you have read. The passage is likely to detail several proposed courses of action and factors affecting these proposals. The reading passage is followed by a conclusion or outcome based on the facts in the passage, or a description of a decision taken regarding the situation. The conclusion is followed by a number of statements that have a possible connection to the conclusion. For each statement, you are to determine whether:

A. The statement proves the conclusion.
B. The statement supports the conclusion but does not prove it.
C. The statement disproves the conclusion.
D. The statement weakens the conclusion but does not disprove it.
E. The statement has no relevance to the conclusion.

Remember that the conclusion after the passage is to be accepted as the outcome of what actually happened, and that you are being asked to evaluate the impact each statement would have had on the conclusion.

PASSAGE:

The Grand Army of Foreign Wars, a national veteran's organization, is struggling to maintain its National Home, where the widowed spouses and orphans of deceased members are housed together in a small village-like community. The Home is open to spouses and children who are bereaved for any reason, regardless of whether the member's death was related to military service, but a new global conflict has led to a dramatic surge in the number of members' deaths: many veterans who re-enlisted for the conflict have been killed in action.

The Grand Army of Foreign Wars is considering several options for handling the increased number of applications for housing at the National Home, which has been traditionally supported by membership dues. At its national convention, it will choose only one of the following:

The first idea is a one-time $50 tax on all members, above and beyond the dues they pay already. Since the organization has more than a million members, this tax should be sufficient for the construction and maintenance of new housing for applicants on the existing grounds of the National Home. The idea is opposed, however, by some older members who live on fixed incomes. These members object in principle to the taxation of Grand Army members. The Grand Army has never imposed a tax on its members.

The second idea is to launch a national fund-raising drive and public relations campaign that will attract donations for the National Home. Several national celebrities are members of the organization, and other celebrities could be attracted to the cause. Many Grand Army members are wary of this approach, however: in the past, the net receipts of some fund-raising efforts have been relatively insignificant, given the costs of staging them.

A third approach, suggested by many of the younger members, is to have new applicants share some of the costs of construction and maintenance. The spouses and children would pay an up-front "enrollment" fee, based on a sliding scale proportionate to their income and assets, and then a monthly fee adjusted similarly to contribute to maintenance costs. Many older members are strongly opposed to this idea, as it is in direct contradiction to the principles on which the organization was founded more than a century ago.

The fourth option is simply to maintain the status quo, focus the organization's efforts on supporting the families who already live at the National Home, and wait to accept new applicants based on attrition.

CONCLUSION: At its annual national convention, the Grand Army of Foreign Wars votes to impose a one-time tax of $10 on each member for the purpose of expanding and supporting the National Home to welcome a larger number of applicants. The tax is considered to be the solution most likely to produce the funds needed to accommodate the growing number of applicants.

10. Actuarial studies have shown that because the Grand Army's membership consists mostly of older veterans from earlier wars, the organization's membership will suffer a precipitous decline in numbers in about five years.

    10.____

    A.
    B.
    C.
    D.
    E.

11. After passage of the funding measure, a splinter group of older members appeals for the "sliding scale" provision to be applied to the tax, so that some members may be allowed to contribute less based on their income.

    11.____

    A.
    B.
    C.
    D.
    E.

12. The original charter of the Grand Army of Foreign Wars specifically states that the organization will not levy any taxes or duties on its members beyond its modest annual dues. It takes a super-majority of attending delegates at the national convention to make alterations to the charter.

    A.
    B.
    C.
    D.
    E.

12.____

13. Six months before Grand Army of Foreign Wars' national convention, the Internal Revenue Service rules that because it is an organization that engages in political lobbying, the Grand Army must no longer enjoy its own federal tax-exempt status.

    A.
    B.
    C.
    D.
    E.

13.____

14. Two months before the national convention, Dirk Rockwell, arguably the country's most famous film actor, announces in a nationally televised interview that he has been saddened to learn of the plight of the National Home, and that he is going to make it his own personal crusade to see that it is able to house and support a greater number of widowed spouses and orphans in the future.

    A.
    B.
    C.
    D.
    E.

14.____

15. The Grand Army's final estimate is that the cost of expanding the National Home to accommodate the increased number of applicants will be about $61 million.

    A.
    B.
    C.
    D.
    E.

15.____

16. Just before the national convention, the federal Department of Veterans Affairs announces steep cuts in the benefits package that is currently offered to the widowed spouses and orphans of veterans.

    A.
    B.
    C.
    D.

16.____

17. After the national convention, the Grand Army of Foreign Wars begins charging a modest "start-up" fee to all families who apply for residence at the national home.

    A.
    B.
    C.
    D.
    E.

17.____

Questions 18-25.

DIRECTIONS: Questions 18-25 each provide four factual statements and a conclusion based on these statements. After reading the entire question, you will decide whether:

    A. The conclusion is proved by statements 1-4;
    B. The conclusion is disproved by statements 1-4; or
    C. The facts are not sufficient to prove or disprove the conclusion.

18. FACTUAL STATEMENTS:

18.____

1. In the Field Day high jump competition, Martha jumped higher than Frank.
2. Carl jumped higher than Ignacio.
3. I gnacio jumped higher than Frank.
4. Dan jumped higher than Carl.

CONCLUSION: Frank finished last in the high jump competition.

    A. The conclusion is proved by statements 1-4.
    B. The conclusion is disproved by statements 1-4.
    C. The facts are not sufficient to prove or disprove the conclusion.

19. FACTUAL STATEMENTS:

19.____

1. The door to the hammer mill chamber is locked if light 6 is red.
2. The door to the hammer mill chamber is locked only when the mill is operating.
3. If the mill is not operating, light 6 is blue.
4. Light 6 is blue.

CONCLUSION: The door to the hammer mill chamber is locked.

    A. The conclusion is proved by statements 1-4.
    B. The conclusion is disproved by statements 1-4.
    C. The facts are not sufficient to prove or disprove the conclusion.

20. FACTUAL STATEMENTS: 20.____

1. Ziegfried, the lion tamer at the circus, has demanded ten additional minutes of performance time during each show.
2. If Ziegfried is allowed his ten additional minutes per show, he will attempt to teach Kimba the tiger to shoot a basketball.
3. If Kimba learns how to shoot a basketball, then Ziegfried was not given his ten additional minutes.
4. Ziegfried was given his ten additional minutes.

CONCLUSION: Despite Ziegfried's efforts, Kimba did not learn how to shoot a basketball.

    A. The conclusion is proved by statements 1-4.
    B. The conclusion is disproved by statements 1-4.
    C. The facts are not sufficient to prove or disprove the conclusion.

21. FACTUAL STATEMENTS: 21.____

1. If Stan goes to counseling, Sara won't divorce him.
2. If Sara divorces Stan, she'll move back to Texas.
3. If Sara doesn't divorce Stan, Irene will be disappointed.
4. Stan goes to counseling.

CONCLUSION: Irene will be disappointed.

    A. The conclusion is proved by statements 1-4.
    B. The conclusion is disproved by statements 1-4.
    C. The facts are not sufficient to prove or disprove the conclusion.

22. FACTUAL STATEMENTS: 22.____

1. If Delia is promoted to district manager, Claudia will have to be promoted to team leader.
2. Delia will be promoted to district manager unless she misses her fourth-quarter sales quota.
3. If Claudia is promoted to team leader, Thomas will be promoted to assistant team leader.
4. Delia meets her fourth-quarter sales quota.

CONCLUSION: Thomas is promoted to assistant team leader.

    A. The conclusion is proved by statements 1-4.
    B. The conclusion is disproved by statements 1-4.
    C. The facts are not sufficient to prove or disprove the conclusion.

23. FACTUAL STATEMENTS: 23.____

    1. Clone D is identical to Clone B.
    2. Clone B is not identical to Clone A.
    3. Clone D is not identical to Clone C.
    4. Clone E is not identical to the clones that are identical to Clone B.

    CONCLUSION: Clone E is identical to Clone D.

    A. The conclusion is proved by statements 1-4.
    B. The conclusion is disproved by statements 1-4.
    C. The facts are not sufficient to prove or disprove the conclusion.

24. FACTUAL STATEMENTS: 24.____

    1. In the Stafford Tower, each floor is occupied by a single business.
    2. Big G Staffing is on a floor between CyberGraphics and MainEvent.
    3. Gasco is on the floor directly below CyberGraphics and three floors above Treehorn
       Audio.
    4. MainEvent is five floors below EZ Tax and four floors below Treehorn Audio.

    CONCLUSION: EZ Tax is on a floor between Gasco and MainEvent.

    A. The conclusion is proved by statements 1-4.
    B. The conclusion is disproved by statements 1-4.
    C. The facts are not sufficient to prove or disprove the conclusion.

25. FACTUAL STATEMENTS: 25.____

    1. Only county roads lead to Nicodemus.
    2. All the roads from Hill City to Graham County are federal highways.
    3. Some of the roads from Plainville lead to Nicodemus.
    4. Some of the roads running from Hill City lead to Strong City.

    CONCLUSION: Some of the roads from Plainville are county roads.

    A. The conclusion is proved by statements 1-4.
    B. The conclusion is disproved by statements 1-4.
    C. The facts are not sufficient to prove or disprove the conclusion.

KEY (CORRECT ANSWERS)

1.	A		11.	A
2.	A		12.	D
3.	A		13.	E
4.	C		14.	D
5.	A		15.	B
6.	B		16.	B
7.	A		17.	C
8.	A		18.	A
9.	A		19.	B
10.	E		20.	A

21.	A
22.	A
23.	B
24.	A
25.	A

———

SOLUTIONS TO PROBLEMS

1) (A) Given statement 3, we deduce that James will not be transferred to another department. By statement 2, we can conclude that James will be promoted.

2) (A) Since every player on the softball team wears glasses, these individuals compose some of the people who work at the bank. Although not every person who works at the bank plays softball, those bank employees who do play softball wear glasses.

3) (A) If Henry and June go out to dinner, we conclude that it must be on Tuesday or Thursday, which are the only two days when they have childbirth classes. This implies that if it is not Tuesday or Thursday, then this couple does not go out to dinner.

4) (C) We can only conclude that if a person plays on the field hockey team, then he or she has both bruises and scarred knees. But there are probably a great number of people who have both bruises and scarred knees but do not play on the field hockey team. The given conclusion can neither be proven or disproven.

5) (A) From statement 1, if Jane beats Mathias, then Lance will beat Jane. Using statement 2, we can then conclude that Christine will not win her match against Jane.

6) (B) Statement 1 tells us that no green light can be an indicator of the belt drive status. Thus, the given conclusion must be false.

7) (A) We already know that Ben and Elliot are in the 7th grade. Even though Hannah and Carl are in the same grade, it cannot be the 7th grade because we would then have at least four students in this 7th grade. This would contradict the third statement, which states that either two or three students are in each grade. Since Amy, Dan, and Francine are in different grades, exactly one of them must be in the 7th grade. Thus, Ben, Elliot and exactly one of Amy, Dan, and Francine are the three students in the 7th grade.

8) (A) One man is a teacher, who is Russian. We know that the writer is female and is Russian. Since her husband is an engineer, he cannot be the Russian teacher. Thus, her husband is of German descent, namely Mr. Stern. This means that Mr. Stern's wife is the writer. Note that one couple consists of a male Russian teacher and a female German lawyer. The other couple consists of a male German engineer and a female Russian writer.

9) (A) Since John is more than 10 inches taller than Lisa, his height is at least 46 inches. Also, John is shorter than Henry, so Henry's height must be greater than 46 inches. Thus, Lisa is the only one whose height is less than 36 inches. Therefore, she is the only one who is not allowed on the flume ride.

18) (A) Dan jumped higher than Carl, who jumped higher than Ignacio, who jumped higher than Frank. Since Martha jumped higher than Frank, every person jumped higher than Frank. Thus, Frank finished last.

19) (B) If the light is red, then the door is locked. If the door is locked, then the mill is operating. Reversing the logical sequence of these statements, if the mill is not operating, then the door is not locked, which means that the light is blue. Thus, the given conclusion is disproved.

20) (A) Using the contrapositive of statement 3, if Ziegfried was given his ten additional minutes, then Kimba did not learn how to shoot a basketball. Since statement 4 is factual, the conclusion is proved.

21) (A) From statements 4 and 1, we conclude that Sara doesn't divorce Stan. Then statement 3 reveals that Irene will be disappointed. Thus the conclusion is proved.

22) (A) Statement 2 can be rewritten as "Delia is promoted to district manager or she misses her sales quota." Furthermore, this statement is equivalent to "If Delia makes her sales quota, then she is promoted to district manager." From statement 1, we conclude that Claudia is promoted to team leader. Finally, by statement 3, Thomas is promoted to assistant team leader. The conclusion is proved.

23) (B) By statement 4, Clone E is not identical to any clones identical to clone B. Statement 1 tells us that clones B and D are identical. Therefore, clone E cannot be identical to clone D. The conclusion is disproved.

24) (A) Based on all four statements, CyberGraphics is somewhere below Main Event. Gasco is one floor below CyberGraphics. EZ Tax is two floors below Gasco. Treehorn Audio is one floor below EZ Tax. Main Event is four floors below Treehorn Audio. Thus, EZ Tax is two floors below Gasco and five floors above Main Event. The conclusion is proved.

25) (A) From statement 3, we know that some of the roads from Plainville lead to Nicodemus. But statement 1 tells us that only county roads lead to Nicodemus. Therefore, some of the roads from Plainville must be county roads. The conclusion is proved.

TEST 2

Questions 1-9.

DIRECTIONS: In questions 1-9, you will read a set of facts and a conclusion drawn from them. The conclusion may be valid or invalid, based on the facts-it's your task to determine the validity of the conclusion.

For each question, select the letter before the statement that BEST expresses the relationship between the given facts and the conclusion that has been drawn from them. Your choices are:
A. The facts prove the conclusion
B. The facts disprove the conclusion; or
C. The facts neither prove nor disprove the conclusion.

1. FACTS: Some employees in the testing department are statisticians. Most of the statisticians who work in the testing department are projection specialists. Tom Wilks works in the testing department.

   CONCLUSION: Tom Wilks is a statistician.

   A. The facts prove the conclusion.
   B. The facts disprove the conclusion.
   C. The facts neither prove nor disprove the conclusion.

1.____

2. FACTS: Ten coins are split among Hank, Lawrence, and Gail. If Lawrence gives his coins to Hank, then Hank will have more coins than Gail. If Gail gives her coins to Lawrence, then Lawrence will have more coins than Hank.

   CONCLUSION: Hank has six coins.

   A. The facts prove the conclusion.
   B. The facts disprove the conclusion.
   C. The facts neither prove nor disprove the conclusion.

2.____

3. FACTS: Nobody loves everybody. Janet loves Ken. Ken loves everybody who loves Janet.

   CONCLUSION: Everybody loves Janet.

   A. The facts prove the conclusion.
   B. The facts disprove the conclusion.
   C. The facts neither prove nor disprove the conclusion.

3.____

4. FACTS: Most of the Torres family lives in East Los Angeles. Many people in East Los   4.____
   Angeles celebrate Cinco de Mayo. Joe is a member of the Torres family.

   CONCLUSION: Joe lives in East Los Angeles.

   A. The facts prove the conclusion.
   B. The facts disprove the conclusion.
   C. The facts neither prove nor disprove the conclusion.

5. FACTS: Five professionals each occupy one story of a five-story office building. Dr.   5.____
   Kane's office is above Dr. Assad's. Dr. Johnson's office is between Dr. Kane's and Dr.
   Conlon's. Dr. Steen's office is between Dr. Conlon's and Dr. Assad's. Dr. Johnson is on
   the fourth story.

   CONCLUSION: Dr. Kane occupies the top story.

   A. The facts prove the conclusion.
   B. The facts disprove the conclusion.
   C. The facts neither prove nor disprove the conclusion.

6. FACTS: To be eligible for membership in the Yukon Society, a person must be able to   6.____
   either tunnel through a snowbank while wearing only a T-shirt and shorts, or hold his
   breath for two minutes under water that is 50° F. Ray can only hold his breath for a
   minute and a half.

   CONCLUSION: Ray can still become a member of the Yukon Society by tunneling
   through a snowbank while wearing a T-shirt and shorts.

   A. The facts prove the conclusion.
   B. The facts disprove the conclusion.
   C. The facts neither prove nor disprove the conclusion.

7. FACTS: A mark is worth five plunks. You can exchange four sharps for a tinplot. It takes   7.____
   eight marks to buy a sharp.

   CONCLUSION: A sharp is the most valuable.

   A. The facts prove the conclusion.
   B. The facts disprove the conclusion.
   C. The facts neither prove nor disprove the conclusion.

8. FACTS: There are gibbons, as well as lemurs, who like to play in the trees at the monkey   8.____
   house. All those who like to play in the trees at the monkey house are fed lettuce and
   bananas.

   CONCLUSION: Lemurs and gibbons are types of monkeys.

   A. The facts prove the conclusion.
   B. The facts disprove the conclusion.
   C. The facts neither prove nor disprove the conclusion.

75

9. FACTS: None of the Blackfoot tribes is a Salishan Indian tribe. Sal-ishan Indians came   9.____
from the northern Pacific Coast. All Salishan Indians live east of the Continental Divide.

CONCLUSION: No Blackfoot tribes live east of the Continental Divide.

    A. The facts prove the conclusion.
    B. The facts disprove the conclusion.
    C. The facts neither prove nor disprove the conclusion.

Questions 10-17.

DIRECTIONS: Questions 10-17 are based on the following reading passage. It is not your knowledge of the particular topic that is being tested, but your ability to reason based on what you have read. The passage is likely to detail several proposed courses of action and factors affecting these proposals. The reading passage is followed by a conclusion or outcome based on the facts in the passage, or a description of a decision taken regarding the situation. The conclusion is followed by a number of statements that have a possible connection to the conclusion. For each statement, you are to determine whether:

    A. The statement proves the conclusion.
    B. The statement supports the conclusion but does not prove it.
    C. The statement disproves the conclusion.
    D. The statement weakens the conclusion but does not disprove it.
    E. The statement has no relevance to the conclusion.

Remember that the conclusion after the passage is to be accepted as the outcome of what actually happened, and that you are being asked to evaluate the impact each statement would have had on the conclusion.

PASSAGE:

On August 12, Beverly Willey reported that she was in the elevator late on the previous evening after leaving her office on the 16th floor of a large office building. In her report, she states that a man got on the elevator at the 11th floor, pulled her off the elevator, assaulted her, and stole her purse. Ms. Willey reported that she had seen the man in the elevators and hallways of the building before. She believes that the man works in the building. Her description of him is as follows: he is tall, unshaven, with wavy brown hair and a scar on his left cheek. He walks with a pronounced limp, often dragging his left foot behind his right.

CONCLUSION: After Beverly Willey makes her report, the police arrest a 43-year-man, Barton Black, and charge him with her assault.

10. Barton Black is a former Marine who served in Vietnam, where he sustained shrapnel   10.____
wounds to the left side of his face and suffered nerve damage in his left leg.

    A.
    B.
    C.
    D.
    E.

11. When they arrived at his residence to question him, detectives were greeted at the door   11._____
    by Barton Black, who was tall and clean-shaven.

    A.
    B.
    C.
    D.
    E.

12. Barton Black was booked into the county jail several days after Beverly Willey's assault.   12._____

    A.
    B.
    C.
    D.
    E.

13. Upon further investigation, detectives discover that Beverly Willey does not work at the   13._____
    office building.

    A.
    B.
    C.
    D.
    E.

14. Upon further investigation, detectives discover that Barton Black does not work at the   14._____
    office building.

    A.
    B.
    C.
    D.
    E.

15. In the spring of the following year, Barton Black is convicted of assaulting Beverly Willey   15._____
    on August 11.

    A.
    B.
    C.
    D.
    E.

16. During their investigation of the assault, detectives determine that Beverly Willey was   16._____
    assaulted on the 12th floor of the office building.

    A.
    B.
    C.
    D.
    E.

17. The day after Beverly Willey's assault, Barton Black fled the area and was never seen   17._____
    again.

    A.
    B.
    C.
    D.
    E.

Questions 18-25.

DIRECTIONS: Questions 18-25 each provide four factual statements and a conclusion based
              on these statements. After reading the entire question, you will decide
              whether:

    A. The conclusion is proved by statements 1-4;
    B. The conclusion is disproved by statements 1-4; or
    C. The facts are not sufficient to prove or disprove the conclusion.

18. FACTUAL STATEMENTS: 18._____

    1. Among five spice jars on the shelf, the sage is to the right of the parsley.
    2. The pepper is to the left of the basil.
    3. The nutmeg is between the sage and the pepper.
    4. The pepper is the second spice from the left.

    CONCLUSION: The sage is the farthest to the right.

    A. The conclusion is proved by statements 1-4.
    B. The conclusion is disproved by statements 1-4.
    C. The facts are not sufficient to prove or disprove the conclusion.

19. FACTUAL STATEMENTS: 19._____

    1. Gear X rotates in a clockwise direction if Switch C is in the OFF position
    2. Gear X will rotate in a counter-clockwise direction if Switch C is ON.
    3. If Gear X is rotating in a clockwise direction, then Gear Y will not be rotating at all.
    4. Switch C is ON.

    CONCLUSION: Gear X is rotating in a counter-clockwise direction.

    A. The conclusion is proved by statements 1-4.
    B. The conclusion is disproved by statements 1-4.
    C. The facts are not sufficient to prove or disprove the conclusion.

20. FACTUAL STATEMENTS: 20.____

    1. Lane will leave for the Toronto meeting today only if Terence, Rourke, and Jackson all file their marketing reports by the end of the work day.
    2. Rourke will file her report on time only if Ganz submits last quarter's data.
    3. If Terence attends the security meeting, he will attend it with Jackson, and they will not file their marketing reports by the end of the work day.
    4. Ganz submits last quarter's data to Rourke.

    CONCLUSION: Lane will leave for the Toronto meeting today.

    A.   The conclusion is proved by statements 1-4.
    B.   The conclusion is disproved by statements 1-4.
    C.   The facts are not sufficient to prove or disprove the conclusion.

21. FACTUAL STATEMENTS: 21.____

    1. Bob is in second place in the Boston Marathon.
    2. Gregory is winning the Boston Marathon.
    3. There are four miles to go in the race, and Bob is gaining on Gregory at the rate of 100 yards every minute.
    4. There are 1760 yards in a mile, and Gregory's usual pace during the Boston Marathon is one mile every six minutes.

    CONCLUSION: Bob wins the Boston Marathon.

    A.   The conclusion is proved by statements 1-4.
    B.   The conclusion is disproved by statements 1-4.
    C.   The facts are not sufficient to prove or disprove the conclusion.

22. FACTUAL STATEMENTS: 22.____

    1. Four brothers are named Earl, John, Gary, and Pete.
    2. Earl and Pete are unmarried.
    3. John is shorter than the youngest of the four.
    4. The oldest brother is married, and is also the tallest.

    CONCLUSION: Gary is the oldest brother.

    A.   The conclusion is proved by statements 1-4.
    B.   The conclusion is disproved by statements 1-4.
    C.   The facts are not sufficient to prove or disprove the conclusion.

23. FACTUAL STATEMENTS: 23.____

    1. Brigade X is ten miles from the demilitarized zone.
    2. If General Woundwort gives the order, Brigade X will advance to the demilitarized zone, but not quickly enough to reach the zone before the conflict begins.
    3. Brigade Y, five miles behind Brigade X, will not advance unless General Woundwort gives the order.
    4. Brigade Y advances.

    CONCLUSION: Brigade X reaches the demilitarized zone before the conflict begins.

A. The conclusion is proved by statements 1-4.
B. The conclusion is disproved by statements 1-4.
C. The facts are not sufficient to prove or disprove the conclusion.

24. FACTUAL STATEMENTS: 24._____

1. Jerry has decided to take a cab from Fullerton to Elverton.
2. Chubby Cab charges $5 plus $3 a mile.
3. Orange Cab charges $7.50 but gives free mileage for the first 5 miles.
4. After the first 5 miles, Orange Cab charges $2.50 a mile.

CONCLUSION: Orange Cab is the cheaper fare from Fullerton to Elverton.

A. The conclusion is proved by statements 1-4.
B. The conclusion is disproved by statements 1-4.
C. The facts are not sufficient to prove or disprove the conclusion.

25. FACTUAL STATEMENTS: 25._____

1. Dan is never in class when his friend Lucy is absent.
2. Lucy is never absent unless her mother is sick.
3. If Lucy is in class, Sergio is in class also
4. Sergio is never in class when Dalton is absent.

CONCLUSION: If Lucy is absent, Dalton may be in class.

A. The conclusion is proved by statements 1-4.
B. The conclusion is disproved by statements 1-4.
C. The facts are not sufficient to prove or disprove the conclusion.

KEY (CORRECT ANSWERS)

1.	C	11.	E
2.	B	12.	B
3.	B	13.	D
4.	C	14.	E
5.	A	15.	A
6.	A	16.	E
7.	B	17.	C
8.	C	18.	B
9.	C	19.	A
10.	B	20.	C

21.	C
22.	A
23.	B
24.	A
25.	B

SOLUTIONS TO PROBLEMS

1) (C) Statement 1 only tells us that some employees who work in the Testing Department are statisticians. This means that we need to allow the possibility that at least one person in this department is not a statistician. Thus, if a person works in the Testing Department, we cannot conclude whether or not this individual is a statistician.

2) (B) If Hank had six coins, then the total of Gails collection and Lawrence's collection would be four. Thus, if Gail gave all her coins to Lawrence, Lawrence would only have four coins. Thus, it would be impossible for Lawrence to have more coins than Hank.

3) (B) Statement 1 tells us that nobody loves everybody. If everybody loved Janet, then Statement 3 would imply that Ken loves everybody. This would contradict statement 1. The conclusion is disproved.

4) (C) Although most of the Torres family lives in East Los Angeles, we can assume that some members of this family do not live in East Los Angeles. Thus, we cannot prove or disprove that Joe, who is a member of the Torres family, lives in East Los Angeles.

5) (A) Since Dr. Johnson is on the 4th floor, either (a) Dr. Kane is on the 5th floor and Dr. Conlon is on the 3rd floor, or (b) Dr. Kane is on the 3rd floor and Dr. Conlon is on the 5th floor. If option (b) were correct, then since Dr. Assad would be on the 1st floor, it would be impossible for Dr. Steen's office to be between Dr. Conlon and Dr. Assad's office. Therefore, Dr. Kane's office must be on the 5th floor. The order of the doctors' offices, from 5th floor down to the 1st floor is: Dr. Kane, Dr. Johnson, Dr. Conlon, Dr. Steen, Dr. Assad.

6) (A) Ray does not satisfy the requirement of holding his breath for two minutes under water, since he can only hold his breath for one minute in that setting. But if he tunnels through a snowbank with just a T-shirt and shorts, he will satisfy the eligibility requirement. Note that the eligibility requirement contains the key word "or." So only one of the two clauses separated by "or" need to be fulfilled.

7) (B) Statement 2 says that four sharps is equivalent to one tinplot. This means that a tinplot is worth more than a sharp. The conclusion is disproved. We note that the order of these items, from most valuable to least valuable are: tinplot, sharp, mark, plunk.

8) (C) We can only conclude that gibbons and lemurs are fed lettuce and bananas. We can neither prove or disprove that these animals are types of monkeys.

9) (C) We know that all Salishan Indians live east of the Continental Divide. But some nonmembers of this tribe of Indians may also live east of the Continental Divide. Since none of the members of the Blackfoot tribe belong to the Salishan Indian tribe, we cannot draw any conclusion about the location of the Blackfoot tribe with respect to the Continental Divide.

18) (B) Since the pepper is second from the left and the nutmeg is between the sage and the pepper, the positions 2, 3, and 4 (from the left) are pepper, nutmeg, sage. By statement 2, the basil must be in position 5, which implies that the parsley is in position 1. Therefore, the basil, not the sage is farthest to the right. The conclusion disproved.

19) (A) Statement 2 assures us that if switch C is ON, then Gear X is rotating in a counterclockwise direction. The conclusion is proved.

20) (C) Based on Statement 4, followed by Statement 2, we conclude that Ganz and Rourke will file their reports on time. Statement 3 reveals that if Terence and Jackson attend the security meeting, they will fail to file their reports on time. We have no further information if Terence and Jackson attended the security meeting, so we are not able to either confirm or deny that their reports were filed on time. This implies that we cannot know for certain that Lane will leave for his meeting in Toronto.

21) (C) Although Bob is in second place behind Gregory, we cannot deduce how far behind Gregory he is running. At Gregory's current pace, he will cover four miles in 24 minutes. If Bob were only 100 yards behind Gregory, he would catch up to Gregory in one minute. But if Bob were very far behind Gregory, for example 5 miles, this is the equivalent of (5)(1760) = 8800 yards. Then Bob would need 8800/100 = 88 minutes to catch up to Gregory. Thus, the given facts are not sufficient to draw a conclusion.

22) (A) Statement 2 tells us that neither Earl nor Pete could be the oldest; also, either John or Gary is married. Statement 4 reveals that the oldest brother is both married and the tallest. By statement 3, John cannot be the tallest. Since John is not the tallest, he is not the oldest. Thus, the oldest brother must be Gary. The conclusion is proved.

23) (B) By statements 3 and 4, General Woundwort must have given the order to advance. Statement 2 then tells us that Brigade X will advance to the demilitarized zone, but not soon enough before the conflict begins. Thus, the conclusion is disproved.

24) (A) If the distance is 5 miles or less, then the cost for the Orange Cab is only $7.50, whereas the cost for the Chubby Cab is $5 + 3x, where x represents the number of miles traveled. For 1 to 5 miles, the cost of the Chubby Cab is between $8 and $20. This means that for a distance of 5 miles, the Orange Cab costs $7.50, whereas the Chubby Cab costs $20. After 5 miles, the cost per mile of the Chubby Cab exceeds the cost per mile of the Orange Cab. Thus, regardless of the actual distance between Fullerton and Elverton, the cost for the Orange Cab will be cheaper than that of the Chubby Cab.

25) (B) It looks like "Dalton" should be replaced by "Dan in the conclusion. Then by statement 1, if Lucy is absent, Dan is never in class. Thus, the conclusion is disproved.

READING COMPREHENSION
UNDERSTANDING AND INTERPRETING WRITTEN MATERIAL
EXAMINATION SECTION
TEST 1

DIRECTIONS: Each question or incomplete statement is followed by several suggested answers or completions. Select the one that BEST answers the question or completes the statement. *PRINT THE LETTER OF THE CORRECT ANSWER IN THE SPACE AT THE RIGHT.*

1. The National Assessment of Educational Progress recently released the results of the first statistically valid national sampling of young adult reading skills in the United States. According to the survey, ninety-five percent of United States young adults (aged 21-25) can read at a fourth-grade level or better. This means they can read well enough to apply for a job, understand a movie guide or join the Army. This is a higher literacy rate than the eighty to eighty-five percent usually estimated for all adults. The study also found that ninety-nine percent can write their names, eighty percent can read a map or write a check for a bill, seventy per cent can understand an appliance warranty or write a letter about a billing error, twenty-five percent can calculate the amount of a tip correctly, and fewer than ten percent can correctly figure the cost of a catalog order or understand a complex bus schedule.

   Which statement about the study is BEST supported by the above passage?

   A. United States literacy rates among young adults are at an all-time high.
   B. Forty percent of young people in the United States cannot write a letter about a billing error.
   C. Twenty percent of United States teenagers cannot read a map.
   D. More than ninety percent of United States young adults cannot correctly calculate the cost of a catalog order.

   1.____

2. It is now widely recognized that salaries, benefits, and working conditions have more of an impact on job satisfaction than on motivation. If they aren't satisfactory, work performance and morale will suffer. But even when they are high, employees will not necessarily be motivated to work well. For example, THE WALL STREET JOURNAL recently reported that as many as forty or fifty percent of newly hired Wall Street lawyers (whose salaries start at upwards of $50,000) quit within the first three years, citing long hours, pressures, and monotony as the prime offenders. It seems there's just not enough of an intellectual challenge in their jobs. An up and coming money-market executive concluded: *Whether it was $1 million or $100 million, the procedure was the same: Except for the tension, a baboon could do my job.* When money and benefits are: adequate, the most important additional determinants of job satisfaction are: more responsibility, a sense of achievement, recognition, and a chance to advance. All of these factors have a more significant influence on employee motivation and performance. As a footnote, several studies have found that the absence of these non-monetary factors can lead to serious stress-related illnesses.

   Which statement is BEST supported by the above passage?

   A. A worker's motivation to perform well is most affected by salaries, benefits, and working conditions.

   2.____

B. Low pay can lead to high levels of job stress.
C. Work performance will suffer if workers feel they are not paid well.
D. After satisfaction with pay and benefits, the next most important factor is more responsibility.

3. The establishment of joint labor-management production committees occurred in the United States during World War I and again during World War II. Their use was greatly encouraged by the National War Labor Board in World War I and the War Production Board in 1942. Because of the war, labor-management cooperation was especially desired to produce enough goods for the war effort, to reduce conflict, and to control inflation. The committees focused on how to achieve greater efficiency, and consulted on health and safety, training, absenteeism, and people issues in general. During the second world war, there were approximately five thousand labor-management committees in factories, affecting over six million workers. While research has found that only a few hundred committees made significant contributions to productivity, there were additional benefits in many cases. It became obvious to many that workers had ideas to contribute to the running of the organization, and that efficient enterprises could become even more so. Labor-management cooperation was also extended to industries that had never experienced it before. Directly after each war, however, few United States labor-management committees were in operation.
Which statement is BEST supported by the above passage?

    3.____

    A. The majority of United States labor-management committees during the second world war accomplished little.
    B. A major goal of United States labor-management committees during the first and second world wars was to increase productivity.
    C. There were more United States labor-management committees during the second world war than during the first world war.
    D. There are few United States labor-management committees in operation today.

4. Studies have found that stress levels among employees who have a great deal of customer contact or a great deal of contact with the public can be very high. There are many reasons for this. Sometimes stress results when the employee is caught in the middle — an organization wants things done one way, but the customer wants them done another way. The situation becomes even worse for the employee's stress levels when he or she knows ways to more effectively provide the service, but isn't allowed to, by the organization. An example is the bank teller who is required to ask a customer for two forms of identification before he or she can cash a check, even though the teller knows the customer well. If organizational mishaps occur or if there are problems with job design, the employee may be powerless to satisfy the customer, and also powerless to protect himself or herself from the customer's wrath. An example of this is the waitress who is forced to serve poorly prepared food. Studies have also found, however, that if the organization and the employee design the positions and the service encounter well, and encourage the use of effective stress management techniques, stress can be reduced to levels that are well below average.
Which statement is BEST supported by the above passage?

    4.____

    A. It is likely that knowledgeable employees will experience greater levels of job-related stress.

B. The highest levels of occupational stress are found among those employees who have a great deal of customer contact.
C. Organizations can contribute to the stress levels of their employees by poorly designing customer contact situations.
D. Stress levels are generally higher in banks and restaurants.

5. It is estimated that approximately half of the United States population suffers from varying degrees of adrenal malfunction. When under stress for long periods of time, the adrenals produce extra cortisol and norepinephrine. By producing more hormones than they were designed to comfortably manufacture and secrete, the adrenals can *burn out over* time and then decrease their secretion. When this happens, the body loses its capacity to cope with stress, and the individual becomes sicker more easily and for longer periods of time. A result of adrenal malfunction may be a diminished output of cortisol. Symptoms of diminished cortisol output include any of the following: craving substances that will temporarily raise serum glucose levels such as caffeine, sweets, soda, juice, or tobacco; becoming dizzy when standing up too quickly; irritability; headaches; and erratic energy levels. Since cortisol is an anti-inflammatory hormone, a decreased output over extended periods of time can make one prone to inflammatory diseases such as arthritis, bursitis, colitis, and allergies. (Many food and pollen allergies disappear when adrenal function is restored to normal.) The patient will have no reserve energy, and infections can spread quickly. Excessive cortisol production, on the other hand, can decrease immunity, leading to frequent and prolonged illnesses.
Which statement is BEST supported by the above passage?

5._____

A. Those who suffer from adrenal malfunction are most likely to be prone to inflammatory diseases such as arthritis and allergies.
B. The majority of Americans suffer from varying degrees of adrenal malfunction.
C. It is better for the health of the adrenals to drink juice instead of soda.
D. Too much cortisol can inhibit the body's ability to resist disease.

6. Psychologist B.F. Skinner pointed out long ago that gambling is reinforced either by design or accidentally, by what he called a variable ratio schedule. A slot machine, for example, is cleverly designed to provide a payoff after it has been played a variable number of times. Although the person who plays it and wins while playing receives a great deal of monetary reinforcement, over the long run the machine will take in much more money than it pays out. Research on both animals and humans has consistently found that such variable reward schedules maintain a very high rate of repeat behavior, and that this behavior is particularly resistant to extinction.
Which statement is BEST supported by the above passage?

6._____

A. Gambling, because it is reinforced by the variable ratio schedule, is more difficult to eliminate than most addictions.
B. If someone is rewarded or wins consistently, even if it is not that often, he or she is likely to continue that behavior.
C. Playing slot machines is the safest form of gambling because they are designed so that eventually the player will indeed win.
D. A cat is likely to come when called if its owner has trained it correctly.

7. Paper entrepreneurialism is an offshoot of scientific management that has become so extreme that it has lost all connection to the actual workplace. It generates profits by cleverly manipulating rules and numbers that only in theory represent real products and real assets. At its worst, paper entrepreneurialism involves very little more than imposing losses on others for the sake of short-term profits. The others may be taxpayers, share holders who end up indirectly subsidizing other share holders, consumers, or investors. Paper entrepreneurialism has replaced product entrepreneurialism, is seriously threatening the United States economy, and is hurting our necessary attempts to transform the nation's industrial and productive economic base. An example is the United States company that complained loudly in 1979 that it did not have the $200 million needed to develop a video-cassette recorder, though demand for them had been very high. The company, however, did not hesitate to spend $1.2 billion that same year to buy a mediocre finance company. The video recorder market was handed over to other countries, who did not hesitate to manufacture them.
Which statement is BEST supported by the above passage?

   A. Paper entrepreneurialism involves very little more than imposing losses on others for the sake of short-term profits.
   B. Shareholders are likely to benefit most from paper entrepreneurialism.
   C. Paper entrepreneurialism is hurting the United States economy.
   D. The United States could have made better video-cassette recorders than the Japanese but we ceded the market to them in 1979.

7.____

8. *The prisoner's dilemma* is an almost 40-year-old game-theory model psychologists, biologists, economists, and political scientists use to try to understand the dynamics of competition and cooperation. Participants in the basic version of the experiment are told that they and their *accomplice* have been caught red-handed. Together, their best strategy is to cooperate by remaining silent. If they do this, each will get off with a 30-day sentence. But either person can do better for himself or herself. If you double-cross your partner, you will go scott free while he or she serves ten years. The problem is, if you each betray the other, you will both go to prison for eight years, not thirty days. No matter what your partner chooses, you are logically better off choosing betrayal. Unfortunately, your partner realizes this too, and so the odds are good that you will both get eight years. That's the dilemma. (The length of the prison sentences is always the same for each variation.) Participants at a recent symposium on behavioral economics at Harvard University discussed the many variations on the game that have been used over the years. In one standard version, subjects are paired with a supervisor who pays them a dollar for each point they score. Over the long run, both subjects will do best if they cooperate every time. Yet in each round, there is a great temptation to betray the other because no one knows what the other will do. The best overall strategy for this variation was found to be *tit for tat*, doing unto your opponent as he or she has just done unto you. It is a simple strategy, but very effective. The partner can easily recognize it and respond. It is retaliatory enough not to be easily exploited, but forgiving enough to allow a pattern of mutual cooperation to develop.
Which statement is BEST supported by the above passage?

   A. The best strategy for playing *prisoner's dilemma* is to cooperate and remain silent.
   B. If you double-cross your partner, and he or she does not double-cross you, your partner will receive a sentence of eight years.

8.____

C.   When playing *prisoner's dilemma*, it is best to double-cross your partner.

D.   If you double-cross your partner, and he or she double-crosses you, you will receive an eight-year sentence.

9.   After many years of experience as the vice president and general manager of a large company, I feel that I know what I'm looking for in a good manager. First, the manager has to be comfortable with himself or herself, and not be arrogant or defensive. Secondly, he or she has to have a genuine interest in people. There are some managers who love ideas — and that's fine — but to be a manager, you must love people, and you must make a hobby of understanding them, believing in them and trusting them. Third, I look for a willingness and a facility to manage conflict. Gandhi defined conflict as a way of getting at the truth. Each person brings his or her own grain of truth and the conflict washes away the illusion and fantasy. Finally, a manager has to have a vision, and the ability and charisma to articulate it. A manager should be seen as a little bit crazy. Some eccentricity is an asset. People don't want to follow vanilla leaders. They want to follow chocolate-fudge-ripple leaders.

9.____

Which statement is BEST supported by the above passage?

A.   It is very important that a good manager spend time studying people.

B.   It is critical for good managers to love ideas.

C.   Managers should try to minimize or avoid conflict.

D.   Managers should be familiar with people's reactions to different flavors of ice cream.

10.   Most societies maintain a certain set of values and assumptions that make their members feel either good or bad about themselves, and either better or worse than other people. In most developed countries, these values are based on the assumption that we are all free to be what we want to be, and that differences in income, work, and education are a result of our own efforts. This may make us believe that people with more income work that is more skilled, more education, and more power are somehow *better* people. We may view their achievements as proof that they have more intelligence, more motivation, and more initiative than those with lower status. The myth tells us that power, income, and education are freely and equally available to all, and that our failure to achieve them is due to our own personal inadequacy. This simply is not the case.

10.____

The possessions we own may also seem to point to our real worth as individuals. The more we own, the more worthy of respect we may feel we are. Or, the acquisition of possessions may be a way of trying to fulfill ourselves, to make up for the loss of community and/or purpose. It is a futile pursuit because lost community and purpose can never be compensated for by better cars or fancier houses. And too often, when these things fail to satisfy, we believe it is only because we don't have enough money to buy better quality items, or more items. We feel bad that we haven't been successful enough to get all that we think we need. No matter how much we do have, goods never really satisfy for long. There is always something else to acquire, and true satisfaction eludes many, many of us.

Which statement is BEST supported by the above passage?

A.   The author would agree with the theory of *survival of the fittest*.

B.   The possessions an individual owns are not a proper measure of his or her real worth.

C. Many countries make a sincere attempt to ensure equal access to quality education for their citizens.
D. The effect a society's value system has on the lives of its members is greatly exag-
gerated.

11. *De nihilo nihil* is Latin *for nothing comes from nothing*. In the first century, the Roman   11.____
poet Persius advised that if anything is to be produced of value, effort must be expended.
He also said, *In nihilum nil posse revorti* - anything once produced cannot become nothing again. It is thought that Persius was parodying Lucretius, who expounded the 500-
year-old physical theories of Epicurus. *De nihilo nihil* can also be used as a cynical comment, to negatively comment on something that is of poor quality produced by a person
of little talent. The implication here is: *What can you expect from such a source?*
Which statement is BEST supported by the above passage?

    A. *In nihilum nil posse revorti* can be interpreted as meaning *if anything is to be pro-
    duced of value, then effort must be expended.*
    B. *De nihilo nihil* can be understood in two different ways.
    C. Lucretius was a great physicist.
    D. Persius felt that Epicurus put in little effort while developing his theories.

12. A Cornell University study has found that less than one percent of the billion pounds of   12.____
pesticides used in this country annually strike their intended targets. The study found that
the pesticides, which are somewhat haphazardly applied to 370 million acres, or about
sixteen percent of the nation's total land area, end up polluting the environment and con-
taminating almost all 200,000 species of plants and animals, including humans. While
the effect of indirect contamination on human cancer rates was not estimated, the study
found that approximately 45,000 human pesticide poisonings occur annually, including
about 3,000 cases admitted to hospitals and approximately 200 fatalities.
Which statement is BEST supported by the above passage?

    A. It is likely that indirect pesticide contamination affects human health.
    B. Pesticides are applied to over one-quarter of the total United States land area.
    C. If pesticides were applied more carefully, fewer pesticide-resistant strains of pests
    would develop.
    D. Human cancer rates in this country would drop considerably if pesticide use was
    cut in half.

13. The new conservative philosophy presents a unified, coherent approach to the world. It   13.____
offers to explain much of our experience since the turbulent 1960s, and it shows what
we've learned since about the dangers of indulgence and permissiveness. But it also
warns that the world has become more ruthless, and that as individuals and as a nation,
we must struggle for survival. It is necessary to impose responsibility and discipline in
order to defeat those forces that threaten us. This lesson is dramatically clear, and can
be applied to a wide range of issues.
Which statement is BEST supported by the above passage?

    A. The 1970s were a time of permissiveness and indulgence.
    B. The new conservative philosophy may help in imposing discipline and a sense of
    responsibility in order to meet the difficult challenges facing this country.
    C. The world faced greater challenges during the second world war than it faces at
    the present time.
    D. More people identify themselves today as conservative in their political philosophy.

14. One of the most puzzling questions in management in recent years has been how usu-   14.____
ally honest, compassionate, intelligent managers can sometimes act in ways that are dis-
honest, uncaring, and unethical. How could top-level managers at the Manville
Corporation, for example, suppress evidence for decades that proved beyond all doubt
that asbestos inhalation was killing their own employees? What drove the managers of a
midwest bank to continue to act in a way that threatened to bankrupt the institution, ruin
its reputation, and cost thousands of employees and investors their jobs and their sav-
ings? It's been estimated that about two out of three of America's five hundred largest
corporations have been involved in some form of illegal behavior. There are, of course,
some common rationalizations used to justify unethical conduct: believing that the activity is in the organization's or the individual's best interest, believing that the activity is not
really immoral or illegal, believing that no one will ever know, or believing that the organization will sanction the behavior because it helps the organization. Ambition can distort
one's sense of *duty*.
Which statement is BEST supported by the above passage?

   A. Top-level managers of corporations are currently involved in a plan to increase eth-
ical behavior among their employees.
   B. There are many good reasons why a manager may act unethically.
   C. Some managers allow their ambitions to override their sense of ethics.
   D. In order to successfully compete, some organizations may have to indulge in
unethical or illegal behavior from time to time.

15. Some managers and supervisors believe that they are leaders because they occupy   15.____
positions of responsibility and authority. But leadership is more than holding a position. It
is often defined in management literature as *the ability to influence the opinions attitudes
and behaviors of others*. Obviously, there are some managers that would not qualify as
leaders, and some leaders that are not *technically* managers. Research has found that
many people overrate their own leadership abilities. In one recent study, seventy percent
of those surveyed rated themselves in the top quartile in leadership abilities, and only
two percent felt they were below average as leaders.
Which statement is BEST supported by the above passage?

   A. In a recent study, the majority of people surveyed rated themselves in the top
twenty-five percent in leadership abilities.
   B. Ninety-eight percent of the people surveyed in a recent study had average or
above-average leadership skills.
   C. In order to be a leader, one should hold a management position.
   D. Leadership is best defined as the ability to be liked by those one must lead.

KEY (CORRECT ANSWERS)

1.	D	6.	B	11.	B
2.	C	7.	C	12.	A
3.	B	8.	D	13.	B
4.	C	9.	A	14.	C
5.	D	10.	B	15.	A

READING COMPREHENSION
UNDERSTANDING AND INTERPRETING WRITTEN MATERIAL
EXAMINATION SECTION
TEST 1

DIRECTIONS: Each question or incomplete statement is followed by several suggested answers or completions. Select the one that BEST answers the question or completes the statement. *PRINT THE LETTER OF THE CORRECT ANSWER IN THE SPACE AT THE RIGHT.*

Questions 1-4.

DIRECTIONS: Questions 1 through 4 are to be answered SOLELY on the basis of the following paragraph.

An annual leave allowance, which combines leaves previously given for vacation, personal business, family illness, and other reasons shall be granted members. Calculation of credits for such leave shall be on an annual basis beginning January 1st of each year. Annual leave credits shall be based on time served by members during preceding calendar year. However, when credits have been accrued and member retires during current year, additional annual leave credits shall, in this instance, be granted at accrual rate of three days for each completed month of service, excluding terminal leave. If accruals granted for completed months of service extend into following month, member shall be granted an additional three days accrual for completed month. This shall be the only condition where accruals in a current year are granted for vacation period in such year.

1. According to the above paragraph, if a fireman's wife were to become seriously ill so that he would take time off from work to be with her, such time off would be deducted from his _____ allowance.

    A. annual leave
    B. vacation leave
    C. personal business leave
    D. family illness leave

1.____

2. Terminal leave means leave taken

    A. at the end of the calendar year
    B. at the end of the vacation year
    C. immediately before retirement
    D. before actually earned, because of an emergency

2.____

3. A fireman appointed on July 1, 2007 will be able to take his first full or normal annual leave during the period

    A. July 1, 2007 to June 30, 2008
    B. Jan. 1, 2008 to Dec. 31, 2008
    C. July 1, 2008 to June 30, 2009
    D. Jan. 1, 2009 to Dec. 31, 2009

3.____

4. According to the above paragraph, a member who retires on July 15 of this year will be entitled to receive leave allowance based on this year of _____ days.

    A. 15   B. 18   C. 22   D. 24

4.____

5. Fire alarm boxes are electromechanical devices for transmitting a coded signal. In each box, there is a trainwork of wheels. When the box is operated, a spring-activated code wheel within begins to revolve. The code number of the box is notched on the circumference of the code wheel, and the latter is associated with the circuit in such a way that when it revolves it causes the circuit to open and close in a predetermined manner, thereby transmitting its particular signal to the central station. A fire alarm box is nothing more than a device for interrupting the flow of current in a circuit in such a way as to produce a coded signal that may be decoded by the dispatchers in the central office.
Based on the above, select the FALSE statement:

    A. Each standard fire alarm box has its own code wheel
    B. The code wheel operates when the box is pulled
    C. The code wheel is operated electrically
    D. Only the break in the circuit by the notched wheel causes the alarm signal to be transmitted to the central office

5.____

Questions 6-9.

DIRECTIONS: Questions 6 through 9 are to be answered SOLELY on the basis of the following paragraph.

Ventilation, as used in fire fighting operations, means opening up a building or structure in which a fire is burning to release the accumulated heat, smoke, and gases. Lack of knowledge of the principles of ventilation on the part of firemen may result in unnecessary punishment due to ventilation being neglected or improperly handled. While ventilation itself extinguishes no fires, when used in an intelligent manner, it allows firemen to get at the fire more quickly, easily, and with less danger and hardship.

6. According to the above paragraph, the MOST important result of failure to apply the principles of ventilation at a fire may be

    A. loss of public confidence
    B. waste of water
    C. excessive use of equipment
    D. injury to firemen

6.____

7. It may be inferred from the above paragraph that the CHIEF advantage of ventilation is that it

    A. eliminates the need for gas masks
    B. reduces smoke damage
    C. permits firemen to work closer to the fire
    D. cools the fire

7.____

8. Knowledge of the principles of ventilation, as defined in the above paragraph, would be LEAST important in a fire in a

    A. tenement house   B. grocery store
    C. ship's hold   D. lumberyard

8.____

9. We may conclude from the above paragraph that for the well-trained and equipped fire-man, ventilation is

    A. a simple matter   B. rarely necessary
    C. relatively unimportant   D. a basic tool

9.____

Questions 10-13.

DIRECTIONS: Questions 10 through 13 are to be answered SOLELY on the basis of the following passage.

Fire exit drills should be established and held periodically to effectively train personnel to leave their working area promptly upon proper signal and to evacuate the building, speedily but without confusion. All fire exit drills should be carefully planned and carried out in a serious manner under rigid discipline so as to provide positive protection in the event of a real emergency. As a general rule, the local fire department should be furnished advance information regarding the exact date and time the exit drill is scheduled. When it is impossible to hold regular drills, written instructions should be distributed to all employees.

Depending upon individual circumstances, fires in warehouses vary from those of fast development that are almost instantly beyond any possibility of employee control to others of relatively slow development where a small readily attackable flame may be present for periods of time up to 15 minutes or more during which simple attack with fire extinguishers or small building hoses may prevent the fire development. In any case, it is characteristic of many warehouse fires that at a certain point in development they flash up to the top of the stack, increase heat quickly, and spread rapidly. There is a degree of inherent danger in attacking warehouse type fires, and all employees should be thoroughly trained in the use of the types of extinguishers or small hoses in the buildings and well instructed in the necessity of always staying between the fire and a direct pass to an exit.

10. Employees should be instructed that, when fighting a fire, they MUST

    A. try to control the blaze
    B. extinguish any fire in 15 minutes
    C. remain between the fire and a direct passage to the exit
    D. keep the fire between themselves and the fire exit

10.____

11. Whenever conditions are such that regular fire drills cannot be held, then which one of the following actions should be taken?

    A. The local fire department should be notified.
    B. Rigid discipline should be maintained during work hours.
    C. Personnel should be instructed to leave their working area by whatever means are available.
    D. Employees should receive fire drill procedures in writing.

11.____

12. The above passage indicates that the purpose of fire exit drills is to train employees to   12.____

    A. control a fire before it becomes uncontrollable
    B. act as firefighters
    C. leave the working area promptly
    D. be serious

13. According to the above passage, fire exit drills will prove to be of UTMOST effectiveness   13.____
if

    A. employee participation is made voluntary
    B. they take place periodically
    C. the fire department actively participates
    D. they are held without advance planning

Questions 14-16.

DIRECTIONS: Questions 14 through 16 are to be answered SOLELY on the basis of the following paragraph.

    The heat output from unit heaters will depend on how fast and how completely dry hot steam fills the unit core. For complete and fast air removal and rapid drainage of condensate, use a trap actuated by water or vapor (inverted bucket trap) and not a trap operated by temperature only (thermostatic or bellows trap). A temperature-actuated trap will hold back the hot condensate until it cools to a point where the thermal element opens. When this happens, the condensate backs up in the heater and reduces the heat output. With a water-actuated trap, this will not happen as the water or condensate is discharged as fast as it is formed.

14. On the basis of the information given in the above paragraph, it can be concluded that   14.____
the PROPER type of trap to use for a unit heater is a(n) _____ trap.

    A. thermostatic   B. bellows-type
    C. inverted bucket   D. temperature

15. According to the above paragraph, the MAIN reason for using the type of trap specified   15.____
for a unit heater is to

    A. bring the condensate up to steam temperature
    B. prevent reduction in the heat output of the unit heater
    C. permit cycling of the heater
    D. maintain constant temperature of condensate in the trap

16. As used in the above paragraph, the word *actuated* means MOST NEARLY   16.____

    A. clogged   B. operated   C. cleaned   D. vented

Question 17 -25.

DIRECTIONS: Questions 17 through 25 are to be answered SOLELY on the basis of the following passage. Each question consists of a statement. You are to indicate whether the statement is TRUE (T) or FALSE (F).

MOVING AN OFFICE

An office with all its equipment is sometimes moved during working hours. This is a difficult task and must be done in an orderly manner to avoid confusion. The operation should be planned in such a way as not to interrupt the progress of work usually done in the office and to make possible the accurate placement of the furniture and records in the new location. If the office moves to a place inside the same building, the desks and files are moved with all their contents. If the movement is to another building, the contents of each desk and file are placed in boxes. Each box is marked with a letter showing the particular section in the new quarters to which it is to be moved. Also marked on each box is the number of the desk or file on which the box is to be placed. Each piece of equipment must have a numbered tag. The number of each piece of equipment is put in soft chalk on the floor in the new office to show the proper location, and several floor plans are made to show where each piece of equipment goes. When the moving is done, someone is stationed at each of the several exits of the old office to see that each box or piece of equipment has its destination clearly marked on it. At the new office, someone stands at each of the several entrances with a copy of the floor plan and directs the placing of the furniture and equipment according to the floor plan. No one should interfere at this point with the arrangements shown on the plan. Improvements in arrangement can be considered and made at a later date.

17. It is a hard job to move an office from one place to another during working hours. 17._____

18. Confusion cannot be avoided if an office is moved during working hours. 18._____

19. The work usually done in an office must be stopped for the day when the office is moved during working hours. 19._____

20. If an office is moved from one floor to another in the same building, the contents of a desk are taken out and put into boxes for moving. 20._____

21. If boxes are used to hold material from desks when moving an office, the box is numbered the same as the desk on which it is to be put. 21._____

22. Letters are marked in soft chalk on the floor at the new quarters to show where the desks should go when moved. 22._____

23. When the moving begins, a person is put at each exit of the old office to check that each box and piece of equipment has clearly marked on it where it to go. 23._____

24. A person stationed at each entrance of the new quarters to direct the placing of the furniture and equipment has a copy of the floor plan of the new quarters. 24._____

25. If, while the furniture is being moved into the new office, a person helping at a doorway gets an idea of a better way to arrange the furniture, he should change the planned arrangement and make a record of the change. 25._____

KEY (CORRECT ANSWERS)

1.	A		11.	D
2.	C		12.	C
3.	D		13.	B
4.	B		14.	C
5.	C		15.	B
6.	D		16.	B
7.	C		17.	T
8.	D		18.	F
9.	D		19.	F
10.	C		20.	F

21.	T
22.	F
23.	T
24.	T
25.	F

―――――

TEST 2

Questions 1-4.

DIRECTIONS: Questions 1 through 4 are to be answered SOLELY on the basis of the following paragraph.

In all cases of homicide, members of the Police Department who investigate will make every effort to obtain statements from dying persons. Such statements are of the greatest importance to the District Attorney. In many cases, there may be a failure to solve the crime if they are not taken. The principal element to be considered in taking the declaration of a dying person is his mental attitude. In order to be admissible in evidence, the person must have no hope of recovery. The patient will be fully interrogated on that point before a statement is taken.

1. In cases of homicide, according to the above paragraph, members of the police force will   1._____

    A.   try to change the mental attitude of the dying person
    B.   attempt to obtain a statement from the dying person
    C.   not give the information they obtain directly to the District Attorney
    D.   be careful not to injure the dying person unnecessarily

2. The mental attitude of the person making the dying statement is of GREAT importance   2._____
    because it can determine, according to the above paragraph, whether the

    A.   victim should be interrogated in the presence of witnesses
    B.   victim will be willing to make a statement of any kind
    C.   statement will tell the District Attorney who committed the crime
    D.   the statement can be used as evidence

3. District Attorneys find that statements of a dying person are important, according to the   3._____
    above paragraph, because

    A.   it may be that the victim will recover and then refuse to testify
    B.   they are important elements in determining the mental attitude of the victim
    C.   they present a point of view
    D.   it may be impossible to punish the criminal without such a statement

4. A well-known gangster is found dying from a bullet wound. The patrolman first on the   4._____
    scene, in the presence of witnesses, tells the man that he is going to die and asks, *Who
    shot you?* The gangster says, *Jones shot me, but he hasn't killed me. I'll live to get him.*
    He then falls back dead. According to the above paragraph, this statement is

    A.   *admissible* in evidence; the man was obviously speaking the truth
    B.   *not admissible* in evidence; the man obviously did not believe that he was dying
    C.   *admissible* in evidence; there were witnesses to the statement
    D.   *not admissible* in evidence; the victim did not sign any statement and the evidence
         is merely hearsay

Questions 5-7.

DIRECTIONS: Questions 5 through 7 are to be answered SOLELY on the basis of the following paragraph.

The factors contributing to crime and delinquency are varied and complex. The home and its immediate environment have been found to be crucial in determining the behavior patterns of the individual, and criminality can frequently be traced to faulty family relationships and a bad neighborhood. But in the search for a clearer understanding of the underlying causes of delinquent and criminal behavior, the total environment must be taken into consideration.

5. According to the above paragraph, family relationships   5._____

    A. tend to become faulty in bad neighborhoods
    B. are important in determining the actions of honest people as well as criminals
    C. are the only important element in the understanding of causes of delinquency
    D. are determined by the total environment

6. According to the above paragraph, the causes of crime and delinquency are   6._____

    A. not simple   B. not meaningless
    C. meaningless   D. simple

7. According to the above paragraph, faulty family relationships FREQUENTLY are   7._____

    A. responsible for varied and complex results
    B. caused when one or both parents have a criminal behavior pattern
    C. independent of the total environment
    D. the cause of criminal acts

Questions 8-10.

DIRECTIONS: Questions 8 through 10 are to be answered SOLELY on the basis of the following paragraph.

A change in the specific problems which confront the police and in the methods for dealing with them has taken place in the last few decades. The automobile is a two-way symbol of this change in policing. It menaces every city with a complicated traffic problem and has speeded up the process of committing a crime and making a getaway, but at the same time has increased the effectiveness of police operations. However, the major concern of police departments continues to be the antisocial or criminal actions and behavior of human beings.

8. On the basis of the above paragraph, it can be stated that, for the most part, in the past   8._____
few decades the specific problems of a police force

    A. have changed but the general problems have not
    B. as well as the general problems have changed
    C. have remained the same but the general problems have changed
    D. as well as the general problems have remained the same

9. According to the above paragraph, advances in science and industry have, in general,   9._____
made the police

    A. operations less effective from the overall point of view
    B. operations more effective from the overall point of view
    C. abandon older methods of solving police problems
    D. concern themselves more with the antisocial acts of human beings

10. The automobile is a *two-way symbol,* according to the above paragraph, because its use   10.____

    A. has speeded up getting to and away from the scene of a crime
    B. both helps and hurts police operations
    C. introduces a new antisocial act—traffic violation—and does away with criminals like horse thieves
    D. both increases and decreases speed by introducing traffic problems

Questions 11-14.

DIRECTIONS: Questions 11 through 14 are to be answered SOLELY on the basis of the following passage on INSTRUCTIONS TO COIN AND TOKEN CASHIERS.

INSTRUCTIONS TO COIN AND TOKEN CASHIERS

Cashiers should reset the machine registers to an even starting number before commencing the day's work. Money bags received directly from collecting agents shall be counted and receipted for on the collecting agent's form. Each cashier shall be responsible for all coin or token bags accepted by him. He must examine all bags to be used for bank deposits for cuts and holes before placing them in use. Care must be exercised so that bags are not cut in opening them. Each bag must be opened separately and verified before another bag is opened. The machine register must be cleared before starting the count of another bag. The amount shown on the machine register must be compared with the amount on the bag tag. The empty bag must be kept on the table for re-examination should there be a difference between the amount on the bag tag and the amount on the machine register.

11. A cashier should BEGIN his day's assignment by   11.____

    A. counting and accepting all money bags
    B. resetting the counting machine register
    C. examining all bags for cuts and holes
    D. verifying the contents of all money bags

12. In verifying the amount of money in the bags received from the collecting agent, it is BEST to   12.____

    A. check the amount in one bag at a time
    B. base the total on the amount on the collecting agent's form
    C. repeat the total shown on the bag tag
    D. refer to the bank deposit receipt

13. A cashier is instructed to keep each empty coin bag on. his table while verifying its contents CHIEFLY because, long as the bag is on the table,   13.____

    A. it cannot be misplaced
    B. the supervisor can see how quickly the cashier works
    C. cuts and holes are easily noticed
    D. a recheck is possible in case the machine count disagrees with the bag tag total

14. The INSTRUCTIONS indicate that it is NOT proper procedure for a cashier to   14._____

    A. assume that coin bags are free of cuts and holes
    B. compare the machine register total with the total shown on the bag tag
    C. sign a form when he receives coin bags
    D. reset the machine register before starting the day's counting

Questions 15-17.

DIRECTIONS: Questions 15 through 17 are to be answered SOLELY on the basis of the following passage.

    The mass media are an integral part of the daily life of virtually every American. Among these media the youngest, television, is the most pervasive. Ninety-five percent of American homes have at least one T.V. set, and on the average that set is in use for about 40 hours each week. The central place of television in American life makes this medium the focal point of a growing national concern over the effects of media portrayals of violence on the values, attitudes, and behavior of an ever increasing audience.

    In our concern about violence and its causes, it is easy to make television a scapegoat. But we emphasize the fact that there is no simple answer to the problem of violence – no single explanation of its causes, and no single prescription for its control. It should be remembered that America also experienced high levels of crime and violence in periods before the advent of television.

    The problem of balance, taste, and artistic merit in entertaining programs on television are complex. We cannot <u>countenance</u> government censorship of television. Nor would we seek to impose arbitrary limitations on programming which might jeopardize television's ability to deal in dramatic presentations with controversial social issues. Nonetheless, we are deeply troubled by television's constant portrayal of violence, not in any genuine attempt to focus artistic expression on the human condition, but rather in pandering to a public preoccupation with violence that television itself has helped to generate.

15. According to the above passage, television uses violence MAINLY   15._____

    A. to highlight the reality of everyday existence
    B. to satisfy the audience's hunger for destructive action
    C. to shape the values and attitudes of the public
    D. when it films documentaries concerning human conflict

16. Which one of the following statements is BEST supported by the above passage?   16._____

    A. Early American history reveals a crime pattern which is not related to television.
    B. Programs should give presentations of social issues and never portray violent acts.
    C. Television has proven that entertainment programs can easily make the balance between taste and artistic merit a simple matter.
    D. Values and behavior should be regulated by governmental censorship.

17. Of the following, which word has the same meaning as *countenance,* as used in the above passage?   17._____

    A. Approve   B. Exhibit   C. Oppose   D. Reject

DIRECTIONS: Questions 18 through 21 are to be answered SOLELY on the basis of the following passage.

Maintenance of leased or licensed areas on public parks or lands has always been a problem. A good rule to follow in the administration and maintenance of such areas is to limit the responsibility of any lessee or licensee to the maintenance of the structures and grounds essential to the efficient operation of the concession, not including areas for the general use of the public, such as picnic areas, public comfort stations, etc.; except where such facilities are leased to another public agency or where special conditions make such inclusion practicable, and where a good standard of maintenance can be assured and enforced. If local conditions and requirements are such that public use areas are included, adequate safeguards to the public should be written into contracts and enforced in their administration, to insure that maintenance by the concessionaire shall be equal to the maintenance standards for other park property.

18. According to the above passage, when an area on a public park is leased to a concessionaire, it is usually BEST to

    A. confine the responsibility of the concessionaire to operation of the facilities and leave the maintenance function to the park agency
    B. exclude areas of general public use from the maintenance obligation of the concessionaire
    C. make the concessionaire responsible for maintenance of the entire area including areas of general public use
    D. provide additional comfort station facilities for the area

18.____

19. According to the above passage, a valid reason for giving a concessionaire responsibility for maintenance of a picnic area within his leased area is that

    A. local conditions and requirements make it practicable
    B. more than half of the picnic area falls within his leased area
    C. the concessionaire has leased picnic facilities to another public agency
    D. the picnic area falls entirely within his leased area

19.____

20. According to the above passage, a precaution that should be taken when a concessionaire is made responsible for maintenance of an area of general public use in a park is

    A. making sure that another public agency has not previously been made responsible for this area
    B. providing the concessionaire with up-to-date equipment, if practicable
    C. requiring that the concessionaire take out adequate insurance for the protection of the public
    D. writing safeguards to the public into the contract

20.____

KEY (CORRECT ANSWERS)

1.	B	11.	B
2.	D	12.	A
3.	D	13.	D
4.	B	14.	A
5.	B	15.	B
6.	A	16.	A
7.	D	17.	A
8.	A	18.	B
9.	B	19.	A
10.	B	20.	D

———

TEST 3

Questions 1-5.

DIRECTIONS: Questions 1 through 5 are to be answered SOLELY on the basis of the following paragraph.

Physical inspections are an important tool for the examiner because he will have to decide the case in many instances on the basis of the inspection report. Most proceedings in a rent office are commenced by the filing of a written application or complaint by an interested party; that is, either the landlord or the tenant. Such an application or complaint must be filed in duplicate in order that the opposing party may be served with a copy of the application or complaint and thus be given an opportunity to answer and oppose it. Sometimes, a further opportunity is given the applicant to file a written rebuttal or reply to his adversary's answer. Often an examiner can make a determination or decision based on the written application, the answer, and the reply to the answer; and, of course, it would speed up operations if it were always possible to make decisions based on written documents only. Unfortunately, decisions can't always be made that way. There are numerous occasions where disputed issues of fact remain which cannot be resolved on the basis of the written statements of the parties. Typical examples are the following: The tenant claims that the refrigerator or stove or bathroom fixture is not functioning properly and the landlord denies this. It is obvious that in such cases an inspection of the accommodations is almost the only means of resolving such disputed issues.

1. According to the above paragraph,

    A. physical inspections are made in all cases
    B. physical inspections are seldom made
    C. it is sometimes possible to determine the facts in a case without a physical inspection
    D. physical inspections are made when it is necessary to verify the examiner's determination

2. According to the above paragraph, in MOST cases, proceedings are started by a(n)

    A. inspector discovering a violation
    B. oral complaint by a tenant or landlord
    C. request from another agency, such as the Building Department
    D. written complaint by a tenant or landlord

3. According to the above paragraph, when a tenant files an application with the rent office, the landlord is

    A. not told about the proceeding until after the examiner makes his determination
    B. given the duplicate copy of the application
    C. notified by means of an inspector visiting the premises
    D. not told about the proceeding until after the inspector has visited the Premises

4. As used in the above paragraph, the word *disputed* means MOST NEARLY

    A. unsettled   B. contested
    C. definite   D. difficult

1.____

2.____

3.____

4.____

5. As used in the above paragraph, the word *resolved* means MOST NEARLY   5.____

   A. settled   B. fixed   C. helped   D. amended

Questions 6-10.

DIRECTIONS: Questions 6 through 10 are to be answered SOLELY on the basis of the follow-
              ing paragraph.

The examiner should order or request an inspection of the housing accommodations. His
request for a physical inspection should be in writing, identify the accommodations and the
landlord and the tenant, and specify precisely just what the inspector is to look for and report
on. Unless this request is specific and lists in detail every item which the examiner wishes to
be reported, the examiner will find that the inspection has not served its purpose and that
even with the inspector's report, he is still in no position to decide the case due to loose ends
which have not been completely tied up. The items that the examiner is interested in should
be separately numbered on the inspection request and the same number referred to in the
inspector's report. You can see what it would mean if an inspector came back with a report
that did not cover everything. It may mean a tremendous waste of time and often require a re-
inspection.

6. According to the above paragraph, the inspector makes an inspection on the order of   6.____

    A. the landlord
    B. the tenant
    C. the examiner
    D. both the landlord and the tenant

7. According to the above paragraph, the reason for numbering each item that an inspector   7.____
    reports on is so that

    A. the report is neat
    B. the report can be easily read and referred to
    C. none of the examiner's requests for information is missed
    D. the report will be specific

8. The one of the following items that is NOT necessarily included in the request for inspec-   8.____
    tion is

    A. location of dwelling   B. name of landlord
    C. item to be checked   D. type of building

9. As used in the above paragraph, the word precisely means MOST NEARLY   9.____

    A. exactly   B. generally   C. Usually   D. strongly

10. As used in the above paragraph, the words in detail mean MOST NEARLY   10.____

     A. clearly   B. item by item
     C. substantially   D. completely

Questions 11-13.

DIRECTIONS: Questions 11 through 13 are to be answered SOLELY on the basis of the following passage.

The agreement under which a tenant rents property from a landlord is known as a lease. Generally speaking, leases are classified as either short-term or long-term in duration. They are further subdivided according to the method used to determine the amount of periodic rent payments. Of the following types of lease in use, the more commonly used ones are the following:

1. The straight or fixed lease is one in which rent may be paid in equal amounts throughout the duration of the lease. These are usually restricted to short-term leasing, or somewhat longer-term if clauses in the lease provide for periodic escalation of payments as the economy shifts.
2. Percentage leasing, used for short-term commercial leasing, provides the landlord with a stipulated percentage of a tenant's gross sales from goods and services sold on the premises, in addition to a fixed amount of rent.
3. The net lease, generally long-term (ten years or more), requires the tenant to pay all operating costs, including real estate taxes and insurance. In a net-net lease, the tenant further agrees to meet mortgage interest and principal payments.
4. An escalated lease, which is a long-term lease, requires rent to be of a stipulated base amount which periodically is subject to escalation in accordance with cost-of-living index scales, or in direct proportion to taxes, insurance, and operating costs.

11. Based on the information given in the passage, which type of lease is MOST likely to be advantageous to a landlord if there is a high rate of inflation? _____ lease.   11._____

    A. Fixed   B. Percentage   C. Net   D. Escalated

12. On the basis of the above passage, which types of lease would generally be MOST suitable for a well-established textile company which requires permanent facilities for its large operations?   12._____
_____ lease and _____ lease.

    A. Percentage; escalated   B. Escalated; net
    C. Straight; net   D. Straight; percentage

13. According to the above passage, the ONLY type of lease which assures the same amount of rent throughout a specified interval is the _____ lease.   13._____

    A. straight   B. percentage   C. net-net   D. escalated

Questions 14-15.

DIRECTIONS: Questions 14 and 15 are to be answered SOLELY on the basis of the following passage.

If you like people, if you seek contact with them rather than hide yourself in a corner, if you study your fellow men sympathetically, if you try consistently to contribute something to their success and happiness, if you are reasonably generous with your thought and your time, if you have a partial reserve with everyone but a seeming reserve with no one, you will get along with your superiors, your subordinates, and the human race.

By the scores of thousands, precepts and platitudes have been written for the guidance of personal conduct. The odd part of it is that, despite all of this labor, most of the frictions in modern society arise from the individual's feeling of inferiority, his false pride, his vanity, his unwillingness to yield space to any other man and his consequent urge to throw his own weight around. Goethe said that the quality which best enables a man to renew his own life, in his relation to others, is his capability of renouncing particular things at the right moment in order warmly to embrace something new in the next.

14. On the basis of the above passage, it may be INFERRED that   14._____

    A. a person should be unwilling to renounce privileges
    B. a person should realize that loss of a desirable job assignment may come at an opportune moment
    C. it is advisable for a person to maintain a considerable amount of reserve in his relationship with unfamiliar people
    D. people should be ready to contribute generously to a worthy charity

15. Of the following, the MOST valid implication made by the above passage is that   15._____

    A. a wealthy person who spends a considerable amount of money entertaining his friends is not really getting along with them
    B. if a person studies his fellow men carefully and impartially, he will tend to have good relationships with them
    C. individuals who maintain seemingly little reserve in their relationships with people have in some measure overcome their own feelings of inferiority
    D. most precepts that have been written for the guidance of personal conduct in relationships with other people are invalid

Questions 16-17.

DIRECTIONS: Questions 16 and 17 are to be answered SOLELY on the basis of the following passage.

When a design for a new bank note of the Federal Government has been prepared by the Bureau of Engraving and Printing and has been approved by the Secretary of the Treasury, the engravers begin the work of cutting the design in steel. No one engraver does all the work. Each man is a specialist. One works only on portraits, another on lettering, another on scroll work, and so on. Each engraver, with a steel tool known as a graver, and aided by a powerful magnifying glass, carefully carves his portion of the design into the steel. He knows that one false cut or a slip of his tool, or one miscalculation of width or depth of line, may destroy the merit of his work. A single mistake means that months or weeks of labor will have been in vain. The Bureau is proud of the fact that no counterfeiter ever has duplicated the excellent work of its expert engravers.

16. According to the above passage, each engraver in the Bureau of Engraving and Printing   16._____

    A. must be approved by the Secretary of the Treasury before he can begin work on the design for a new bank note
    B. is responsible for engraving a complete design of a new bank note by himself
    C. designs new bank notes and submits them for approval to the Secretary of the Treasury
    D. performs only a specific part of the work of engraving a design for a new bank note

17. According to the above passage,　　　　　　　　　　　　　　　　　　17._____

 A. an engraver's tools are not available to a counterfeiter
 B. mistakes made in engraving a design can be corrected immediately with little delay in the work of the Bureau
 C. the skilled work of the engravers has not been successfully reproduced by counterfeiter
 D. careful carving and cutting by the engravers is essential to prevent damage to equipment

Questions 18-21.

DIRECTIONS: Questions 18 through 21 are to be answered SOLELY on the basis of the following passage.

In the late fifties, the average American housewife spent $4.50 per day for a family of four on food and 5.15 hours in food preparation, if all of her food was *home prepared;* she spent $5.80 per day and 3.25 hours if all of her food was purchased *partially prepared;* and $6.70 per day and 1.65 hours if all of her food was purchased *ready to serve.*

Americans spent about 20 billion dollars for food products in 1941. They spent nearly 70 billion dollars in 1958. They spent 25 percent of their cash income on food in 1958. For the same kinds and quantities of food that consumers bought in 1941, they would have spent only 16% of their cash income in 1958. It is obvious that our food does cost more. Many factors contribute to this increase besides the additional cost that might be attributed to processing. Consumption of more expensive food items, higher marketing margins, and more food eaten in restaurants are other factors.

The Census of Manufacturers gives some indication of the total bill for processing. The value added by manufacturing of food and kindred products amounted to 3.5 billion of the 20 billion dollars spent for food in 1941. In the year 1958, the comparable figure had climbed to 14 billion dollars.

18. According to the above passage, the cash income of Americans in 1958 was MOST 18._____
NEARLY _____ billion dollars.

 A. 11.2   B. 17.5   C. 70   D. 280

19. According to the above passage, if Americans bought the same kinds and quantities of 19._____
food in 1958 as they did in 1941, they would have spent MOST NEARLY _____ billion dollars.

 A. 20   B. 45   C. 74   D. 84

20. According to the above passage, the percent increase in money spent for food in 1958 20._____
over 1941, as compared with the percentage increase in money spent for food processing in the same years,

 A. was greater
 B. was less
 C. was the same
 D. cannot be determined from the passage

21. In 1958, an American housewife who bought all of her food ready-to-serve saved in time, 21.____
    as compared with the housewife who prepared all of her food at home

    A. 1.6 hours daily
    B. 1.9 hours daily
    C. 3.5 hours daily
    D. an amount of time which cannot be determined from the above passage

Questions 22-25.

DIRECTIONS: Questions 22 through 25 are to be answered SOLELY on the basis of the fol-
             lowing passage.

Any member of the retirement system who is in city service, who files a proper application for service credit and agrees to deductions from his compensation at triple his normal
rate of contribution, shall be credited with a period of city service previous to the beginning of
his present membership in the retirement system. The period of service credited shall be
equal to the period throughout which such triple deductions are made, but may not exceed
the total of the city service the member rendered between his first day of eligibility for membership in the retirement system and the day he last became a member. After triple contributions for all of the first three years of service credit claimed, the remaining service credit may
be purchased by a single payment of the sum of the remaining payments. If the total time pur-
chasable exceeds ten years, triple contributions may be made for one-half of such time, and
the remaining time purchased by a single payment of the sum of the remaining payments.
Credit for service acquired in the above manner may be used only in determining the amount
of any retirement benefit. Eligibility for such benefit will, in all cases, be based upon service
rendered after the employee's membership last began, and will be exclusive of service credit
purchased as described below.

22. According to the above passage, in order to obtain credit for city service previous to the 22.____
    beginning of an employee's present membership in the retirement system, the employee
    must

    A. apply for the service credit and consent to additional contributions to the retirement
       system
    B. apply for the service credit before he renews his membership in the retirement sys-
       tem
    C. have previous city service which does not exceed ten years
    D. make contributions to the retirement system for three years

23. According to the information in the above passage, credit for city service previous to the 23.____
    beginning of an employee's present membership in the retirement system, is

    A. credited up to a maximum of ten years
    B. credited to any member of the retirement system
    C. used in determining the amount of the employee's benefits
    D. used in establishing the employee's eligibility to receive benefits

24. According to the information in the above passage, a member of the retirement system   24.____
may purchase service credit for

    A. the period of time between his first day of eligibility for membership in the retirement system and the date he applies for the service credit
    B. one-half of the total of his previous city service if the total time exceeds ten years
    C. the period of time throughout which triple deductions are made
    D. the period of city service between his first day of eligibility for membership in the retirement system and the day he last became a member

25. Suppose that a member of the retirement system has filed an application for service   25.____
credit for five years of previous city service.
Based on the information in the above passage, the employee may purchase credit for
this previous city service by making

    A. triple contributions for three years
    B. triple contributions for one-half of the time and a single payment of the sum of the remaining payments
    C. triple contributions for three years and a single payment of the sum of the remaining payments
    D. a single payment of the sum of the payments

KEY (CORRECT ANSWERS)

1.	C		11.	D
2.	D		12.	B
3.	B		13.	A
4.	B		14.	B
5.	A		15.	C
6.	C		16.	D
7.	C		17.	C
8.	D		18.	D
9.	A		19.	B
10.	B		20.	B

21.	C
22.	A
23.	C
24.	D
25.	C

PREPARING WRITTEN MATERIAL

PARAGRAPH REARRANGEMENT
COMMENTARY

The sentences which follow are in scrambled order. You are to rearrange them in proper order and indicate the letter choice containing the correct answer at the space at the right.

Each group of sentences in this section is actually a paragraph presented in scrambled order. Each sentence in the group has a place in that paragraph; no sentence is to be left out. You are to read each group of sentences and decide upon the best order in which to put the sentences so as to form as well-organized paragraph.

The questions in this section measure the ability to solve a problem when all the facts relevant to its solution are not given.

More specifically, certain positions of responsibility and authority require the employee to discover connections between events sometimes, apparently, unrelated. In order to do this, the employee will find it necessary to correctly infer that unspecified events have probably occurred or are likely to occur. This ability becomes especially important when action must be taken on incomplete information.

Accordingly, these questions require competitors to choose among several suggested alternatives, each of which presents a different sequential arrangement of the events. Competitors must choose the MOST logical of the suggested sequences.

In order to do so, they may be required to draw on general knowledge to infer missing concepts or events that are essential to sequencing the given events. Competitors should be careful to infer only what is essential to the sequence. The plausibility of the wrong alternatives will always require the inclusion of unlikely events or of additional chains of events which are NOT essential to sequencing the given events.

It's very important to remember that you are looking for the best of the four possible choices, and that the best choice of all may not even be one of the answers you're given to choose from.

There is no one right way to solve these problems. Many people have found it helpful to first write out the order of the sentences, as they would have arranged them, on their scrap paper before looking at the possible answers. If their optimum answer is there, this can save them some time. If it isn't, this method can still give insight into solving the problem. Others find it most helpful to just go through each of the possible choices, contrasting each as they go along. You should use whatever method feels comfortable, and works, for you.

While most of these types of questions are not that difficult, we've added a higher percentage of the difficult type, just to give you more practice. Usually there are only one or two questions on this section that contain such subtle distinctions that you're unable to answer confidently, and you then may find yourself stuck deciding between two possible choices, neither of which you're sure about.

Preparing Written Material

EXAMINATION SECTION
TEST 1

DIRECTIONS: The following groups of sentences need to be arranged in an order that makes sense. Select the letter preceding the sequence that represents the best sentence order. *PRINT THE LETTER OF THE CORRECT ANSWER IN THE SPACE AT THE RIGHT.*

Question 1

1.____

1. The ostrich egg shell's legendary toughness makes it an excellent substitute for certain types of dishes or dinnerware, and in parts of Africa ostrich shells are cut and decorated for use as containers for water.
2. Since prehistoric times, people have used the enormous egg of the ostrich as a part of their diet, a practice which has required much patience and hard work-to hard-boil an ostrich egg takes about four hours.
3. Opening the egg's shell, which is rock hard and nearly an inch thick, requires heavy tools, such as a saw or chisel; from inside, a baby ostrich must use a hornlike projection on its beak as a miniature pick-axe to escape from the egg.
4. The offspring of all higher-order animals originate from single egg cells that are carried by mothers, and most of these eggs are relatively small, often microscopic.
5. The egg of the African ostrich, however, weighs a massive thirty pounds, making it the largest single cell on earth, and a common object of human curiosity and wonder.

The best order is

A. 5 4 1 2 3
B. 1 4 5 3 2
C. 4 2 3 5 1
D. 4 5 2 3 1

Question 2

2.____

1. Typically only a few feet high on the open sea, individual tsunami have been known to circle the entire globe two or three times if their progress is not interrupted, but are not usually dangerous until they approach the shallow water that surrounds land masses.
2. Some of the most terrifying and damaging hazards caused by earthquakes are tsunami, which were once called "tidal waves"— a poorly chosen name, since these waves have nothing to do with tides.
3. Then a wave, slowed by the sudden drag on the lower part of its moving water column, will pile upon itself, sometimes reaching a height of over 100 feet.
4. Tsunami (Japanese for "great harbor wave") are seismic waves that are caused by earthquakes near oceanic trenches, and once triggered, can travel up to 600 miles an hour on the open ocean.
5. A land-shoaling tsunami is capable of extraordinary destruction; some tsunami have deposited large boats miles inland, washed out two-foot-thick seawalls, and scattered locomotive trains over long distances.

The best order is

A. 4 1 3 2 5
B. 1 3 4 2 5
C. 5 1 3 2 4
D. 2 4 1 3 5

Question 3   3.____

1. Soon, by the 1940's, jazz was the most popular type of music among American intellectu-
    als and college students.
2. In the early days of jazz, it was considered "lowdown" music, or music that was played only
    in rough, disreputable bars and taverns.
3. However, jazz didn't take long to develop from early ragtime melodies into more complex,
    sophisticated forms, such as Charlie Parker's "bebop" style of jazz.
4. After charismatic band leaders such as Duke Ellington and Count Basic brought jazz to a
    larger audience, and jazz continued to evolve into more complicated forms, white audi-
    ences began to accept and even to enjoy the new American art form.
5. Many white Americans, who then dictated the tastes of society, were wary of music that
    was played almost exclusively in black clubs in the poorer sections of cities and towns.

The best order is

A. 5 4 3 2 1
B. 2 5 3 4 1
C. 4 5 3 1 2
D. 1 2 4 3 5

Question 4   4.____

1. Then, hanging in a windless place, the magnetized end of the needle would always point to
    the south.
2. The needle could then be balanced on the rim of a cup, or the edge of a fingernail, but this
    balancing act was hard to maintain, and the needle often fell off.
3. Other needles would point to the north, and it was important for any traveler finding his way
    with a compass to remember which kind of magnetized needle he was carrying.
4. To make some of the earliest compasses in recorded history, ancient Chinese "magicians"
    would rub a needle with a piece of magnetized iron called a lodestone.
5. A more effective method of keeping the needle free to swing with its magnetic pull was to
    attach a strand of silk to the center of the needle with a tiny piece of wax.

The best order is

A. 4 2 5 1 3
B. 4 3 5 2 1
C. 4 5 2 1 3
D. 4 1 3 5 2

Question 5

1. The now-famous first mate of the *HMS Bounty,* Fletcher Christian, founded one of the world's most peculiar civilizations in 1790.
2. The men knew they had just committed a crime for which they could be hanged, so they set sail for Pitcairn, a remote, abandoned island in the far eastern region of the Polynesian archipelago, accompanied by twelve Polynesian women and six men.
3. In a mutiny that has become legendary, Christian and the others forced Captain Bligh into a lifeboat and set him adrift off the coast of Tonga in April of 1789.
4. In early 1790, the *Bounty* landed at Pitcairn Island, where the men lived out the rest of their lives and founded an isolated community which to this day includes direct descendants of Christian and the other crewmen.
5. The *Bounty,* commanded by Captain William Bligh, was in the middle of a global voyage, and Christian and his shipmates had come to the conclusion that Bligh was a reckless madman who would lead them to their deaths unless they took the ship from him.

The best order is

A.   4 5 3 2 1
B.   1 3 5 2 4
C.   1 5 3 2 4
D.   3 1 5 4 2

Question 6

6

1. But once the vines had been led to make orchids, the flowers had to be carefully hand-pollinated, because unpollinated orchids usually lasted less than a day, wilting and dropping off the vine before it had even become dark.
2. The Totonac farmers discovered that looping a vine back around once it reached a five-foot height on its host tree would cause the vine to flower.
3. Though they knew how to process the fruit pods and extract vanilla's flavoring agent, the Totonacs also knew that a wild vanilla vine did not produce abundant flowers or fruit.
4. Wild vines climbed along the trunks and canopies of trees, and this constant upward growth diverted most of the vine's energy to making leaves instead of the orchid flowers that, once pollinated, would produce the flavorful pods.
5. Hundreds of years before vanilla became a prized food flavoring in Europe and the Western World, the Totonac Indians of the Mexican Gulf Coast were skilled cultivators of the vanilla vine, whose fruit they literally worshipped as a goddess.

The best order is

A.   2 3 4 1 5
B.   2 4 3 1 5
C.   5 3 4 2 1
D.   3 4 1 2 5

Question 7

7.____

1. Once airborne, the spider is at the mercy of the air currents—usually the spider takes a brief journey, traveling close to the ground, but some have been found in air samples collected as high as 10,000 feet, or been reported landing on ships far out at sea.
2. Once a young spider has hatched, it must leave the environment into which it was born as quickly as possible, in order to avoid competing with its hundreds of brothers and sisters for food.
3. The silk rises into warm air currents, and as soon as the pull feels adequate the spider lets go and drifts up into the air, suspended from the silk strand in the same way that a person might parasail.
4. To help young spiders do this, many species have adapted a practice known as "aerial dispersal," or, in common speech, "ballooning."
5. A spider that wants to leave its surroundings quickly will climb to the top of a grass stem or twig, face into the wind, and aim its back end into the air, releasing a long stream of silk from the glands near the tip of its abdomen.

The best order is

    A. 5 4 2 3 1
    B. 5 2 4 1 3
    C. 2 5 4 3 1
    D. 2 4 5 3 1

Question 8

8.____

1. For about a year, Tycho worked at a castle in Prague with a scientist named Johannes Kepler, but their association was cut short by another argument that drove Kepler out of the castle, to later develop, on his own, the theory of planetary orbits.
2. Tycho found life without a nose embarrassing, so he made a new nose for himself out of silver, which reportedly remained glued to his face for the rest of his life.
3. Tycho Brahe, the 17th-century Danish astronomer, is today more famous for his odd and arrogant personality than for any contribution he has made to our knowledge of the stars and planets.
4. Early in his career, as a student at Rostock University, Tycho got into an argument with the another student about who was the better mathematician, and the two became so angry that the argument turned into a sword fight, during which Tycho's nose was sliced off.
5. Later in his life, Tycho's arrogance may have kept him from playing a part in one of the greatest astronomical discoveries in history: the elliptical orbits of the solar system's planets.

The best order is

    A. 1 4 2 3 5
    B. 4 2 3 5 1
    C. 4 2 1 3 5
    D. 3 4 2 5 1

Question 9

9._____

1. The processionaries are so used to this routine that if a person picks up the end of a silk line and brings it back to the origin—creating a closed circle—the caterpillars may travel around and around for days, sometimes starving ar freezing, without changing course.
2. Rather than relying on sight or sound, the other caterpillars, who are lined up end-to-end behind the leader, travel to and from their nests by walking on this silk line, and each will reinforce it by laying down its own marking line as it passes over.
3. In order to insure the safety of individuals, the processionary caterpillar nests in a tree with dozens of other caterpillars, and at night, when it is safest, they all leave together in search of food.
4. The processionary caterpillar of the European continent is a perfect illustration of how much some insect species rely on instinct in their daily routines.
5. As they leave their nests, the processionaries form a single-file line behind a leader who spins and lays out a silk line to mark the chosen path.

The best order is

A. 4 3 5 2 1
B. 3 5 4 2 1
C. 3 5 2 1 4
D. 4 5 3 1 2

Question 10

10._____

1. Often, the child is also given a handcrafted walker or push cart, to provide support for its first upright explorations.
2. In traditional Indian families, a child's first steps are celebrated as a ceremonial event, rooted in ancient myth.
3. These carts are often intricately designed to resemble the chariot of Krishna, an important figure in Indian mythology.
4. The sound of these anklet bells is intended to mimic the footsteps of the legendary child Rama, who is celebrated in devotional songs throughout India.
5. When the child's parents see that the child is ready to begin walking, they will fit it with specially designed ankle bracelets, adorned with gently ringing bells.

The best order is

A. 2 3 4 1 5
B. 2 5 3 1 4
C. 5 4 1 3 2
D. 5 3 2 1 4

Question 11   11.____

1. The settlers planted Osage orange all across Middle America, and today long lines and rectangles of Osage orange trees can still be seen on the prairies, running along the former boundaries of farms that no longer exist.
2. After trying sod walls and water-filled ditches with no success, American farmers began to look for a plant that was adaptable to prairie weather, and that could be trimmed into a hedge that was "pig-tight, horse-high, and bull-strong."
3. The tree, so named because it bore a large (but inedible) fruit the size of an orange, was among the sturdiest and hardiest of American trees, and was prized among Native Americans for the strength and flexibility of bows which were made from its wood.
4. The first people to practice agriculture on the American flatlands were faced with an important problem: what would they use to fence their land in a place that was almost entirely without trees or rocks?
5. Finally, an Illinois farmer brought the settlers a tree that was native to the land between the Red and Arkansas rivers, a tree called the Osage orange.

The best order is

A. 2 1 5 3 4
B. 1 2 3 4 5
C. 4 2 5 3 1
D. 4 2 1 3 5

Question 12   12.____

1. After about ten minutes of such spirited and complicated activity, the head dancer is free to make up his or her own movements while maintaining the interest of the New Year's crowd.
2. The dancer will then perform a series of leg kicks, while at the same time operating the lion's mouth with his own hand and moving the ears and eyes by means of a string which is attached to the dancer's own mouth.
3. The most difficult role of this dance belongs to the one who controls the lion's head; this person must lead all the other "parts" of the lion through the choreographed segments of the dance.
4. The head dancer begins with a complex series of steps, alternately stepping forward with the head raised, and then retreating a few steps while lowering the head, a movement that is intended to create the impression that the lion is keeping a watchful eye for anything evil.
5. When performing a traditional Chinese New Year's lion dance, several performers must fit themselves inside a large lion costume and work together to enact different parts of the dance.

The best order is

A. 5 3 4 2 1
B. 3 4 2 5 1
C. 3 1 5 4 2
D. 4 2 3 5 1

Question 13

13

1. For many years the shell of the chambered nautilus was treasured in Europe for its beauty and intricacy, but collectors were unaware that they were in possession of the structure that marked a "missing link" in the evolution of marine mollusks.
2. The nautilus, however, evolved a series of enclosed chambers in its shell, and invented a new use for the structure: the shell began to serve as a buoyancy device.
3. Equipped with this new flotation device, the nautilus did not need the single, muscular foot of its predecessors, but instead developed flaps, tentacles, and a gentle form of jet propulsion that transformed it into the first mollusk able to take command of its own destiny and explore a three-dimensional world.
4. By pumping and adjusting air pressure into the chambers, the nautilus could spend the day resting on the bottom, and then rise toward the surface at night in search of food.
5. The nautilus shell looks like a large snail shell, similar to those of its ancestors, who used their shells as protective coverings while they were anchored to the sea floor.

The best order is

A. 5 2 4 1 3
B. 5 1 2 3 4
C. 1 2 5 3 4
D. 1 5 2 4 3

Question 14

14

1. While France and England battled for control of the region, the Acadiens prospered on the fertile farmland, which was finally secured by England in 1713.
2. Early in the 17th century, settlers from western France founded a colony called Acadie in what is now the Canadian province of Nova Scotia.
3. At this time, English officials feared the presence of spies among the Acadiens who might be loyal to their French homeland, and the Acadiens were deported to spots along the Atlantic and Caribbean shores of America.
4. The French settlers remained on this land, under English rule, for around forty years, until the beginning of the French and Indian War, another conflict between France and England.
5. As the Acadien refugees drifted toward a final home in southern Louisiana, neighbors shortened their name to "Cadien," and finally "Cajun," the name which the descendants of early Acadiens still call themselves.

The best order is

A. 1 4 2 3 5
B. 2 1 3 5 4
C. 2 1 4 3 5
D. 5 2 3 4 1

Question 15

15.____

1. Traditional households in the Eastern and Western regions of Africa serve two meals a day-one at around noon, and the other in the evening.
2. The starch is then used in the way that Americans might use a spoon, to scoop up a portion of the main dish on the person's plate.
3. The reason for the starch's inclusion in every meal has to do with taste as well as nutrition; African food can be very spicy, and the starch is known to cool the burning effect of the main dish.
4. When serving these meals, the main dish is usually served on individual plates, and the starch is served on a communal plate, from which diners break off a piece of bread or scoop rice or fufu in their fingers.
5. The typical meals usually consist of a thick stew or soup as the main course, and an accompanying starch—either bread, rice, *or fufu, a* starchy grain paste similar in consistency to mashed potatoes.

The best order is

A. 5 2 3 4 1
B. 5 1 4 3 2
C. 1 4 5 3 2
D. 1 5 4 2 3

Question 16

16.____

1. In the early days of the American Midwest, Indiana settlers sometimes came together to hold an event called an apple peeling, where neighboring settlers gathered at the homestead of a host family to help prepare the hosts' apple crop for cooking, canning, and making apple butter.
2. At the beginning of the event, each peeler sat down in front of a ten- or twenty-gallon stone jar and was given a crock of apples and a paring knife.
3. Once a peeler had finished with a crock, another was placed next to him; if the peeler was an unmarried man, he kept a strict count of the number of apples he had peeled, because the winner was allowed to kiss the girl of his choice.
4. The peeling usually ended by 9:30 in the evening, when the neighbors gathered in the host family's parlor for a dance social.
5. The apples were peeled, cored, and quartered, and then placed into the jar.

The best order is

A. 1 5 3 4 2
B. 2 5 3 4 1
C. 1 2 5 3 4
D. 2 1 5 4 3

Question 17

17.____

1. If your pet turtle is a land turtle and is native to temperate climates, it will stop eating some time in October, which should be your cue to prepare the turtle for hibernation.
2. The box should then be covered with a wire screen, which will protect the turtle from any rodents or predators that might want to take advantage of a motionless and helpless animal.
3. When your turtle hasn't eaten for a while and appears ready to hibernate, it should be moved to its winter quarters, most likely a cellar or garage, where the temperature should range between 40° and 45° F.
4. Instead of feeding the turtle, you should bathe it every day in warm water, to encourage the turtle to empty its intestines in preparation for its long winter sleep.
5. Here the turtle should be placed in a well-ventilated box whose bottom is covered with a moisture-absorbing layer of clay beads, and then filled three-fourths full with almost dry peat moss or wood chips, into which the turtle will burrow and sleep for several months.

The best order is

  A. 1 4 3 5 2
  B. 3 4 2 5 1
  C. 3 2 4 1 5
  D. 4 5 2 3 1

Question 18

18.____

1. Once he has reached the nest, the hunter uses two sturdy bamboo poles like huge chopsticks to pull the nest away from the mountainside, into a large basket that will be lowered to people waiting below.
2. The world's largest honeybees colonize the Nepalese mountainsides, building honeycombs as large as a person on sheer rock faces that are often hundreds of feet high.
3. In the remote mountain country of Nepal, a small band of "honey hunters" carry out a tradition so ancient that 10,000 year-old drawings of the practice have been found in the caves of Nepal.
4. To harvest the honey and beeswax from these combs, a honey hunter climbs above the nests, lowers a long bamboo-fiber ladder over the cliff, and then climbs down.
5. Throughout this dangerous practice, the hunter is stung repeatedly, and only the veterans, with skin that has been toughened over the years, are able to return from a hunt without the painful swelling caused by stings.

The best order is

  A. 2 4 3 5 1
  B. 2 4 1 5 3
  C. 5 3 2 4 1
  D. 3 2 4 1 5

Question 19

19

1. After the Romans left Britain, there were relentless attacks on the islands from the barbarian tribes of northern Germany—the Angles, Saxons, and Jutes.
2. As the empire weakened, Roman soldiers withdrew from Britain, leaving behind a country that continued to practice the Christian religion that had been introduced by the Romans.
3. Early Latin writings tell of a Christian warrior named Arturius (Arthur, in English) who led the British citizens to defeat these barbarian invaders, and brought an extended period of peace to the lands of Britain.
4. Long ago, the British Isles were part of the far-flung Roman Empire that extended across most of Europe and into Africa and Asia.
5. The romantic legend of King Arthur and his knights of the Round Table, one of the most popular and widespread stories of all time, appears to have some foundation in history.

The best order is

A. 5 4 3 2 1
B. 5 4 2 1 3
C. 4 5 2 3 1
D. 4 3 2 1 5

Question 20

20

1. The cylinder was allowed to cool until it sould stand on its own, and then it was cut from the tube and split down the side with a single straight cut.
2. Nineteenth-century glassmakers, who had not yet discovered the glazier's modern techniques for making panes of glass, had to create a method for converting their blown glass into flat sheets.
3. The bubble was then pierced at the end to make a hole that opened up while the glassmaker gently spun it, creating a cylinder of glass.
4. Turned on its side and laid on a conveyor belt, the cylinder was strengthened, or tempered, by being heated again and cooled very slowly, eventually flattening out into a single rectangular piece of glass.
5. To do this, the glassmaker dipped the end of a long tube into melted glass and blew into the other end of the tube, creating an expanding bubble of glass.

The best order is

A. 2 5 3 4 1
B. 2 4 5 3 1
C. 3 5 2 4 1
D. 3 1 4 5 2

Question 21

   1. The splints are almost always hidden, but horses are occasionally born whose splinted toes project from the leg on either side, just above the hoof.

   2. The second and fourth toes remained, but shrank to thin splints of bone that fused invisibly to the horse's leg bone.

   3. Horses are unique among mammals, having evolved feet that each end in what is essentially a single toe, capped by a large, sturdy hoof.

   4. Julius Caesar, an emperor of ancient Rome, was said to have owned one of these three-toed horses, and considered it so special that he would not permit anyone else to ride it.

   5. Though the horse's earlier ancestors possessed the traditional mammalian set of five toes on each foot, the horse has retained only its third toe; its first and fifth toes disappeared completely as the horse evolved.

The best order is

   A. 3 5 2 1 4
   B. 5 3 2 4 1
   C. 3 2 5 1 4
   D. 5 2 3 1 4

Question 22

   1. The new building materials—some of which are twenty feet long, and weigh nearly six tons—were transported to Pohnpei on rafts, and were brought into their present position by using hibiscus fiber ropes and leverage to move the stone columns upward along the inclined trunks of coconut palm trees.

   2. The ancestors built great fires to heat the stone, and then poured cool seawater on the columns, which caused the stone to contract and split along natural fracture lines.

   3. The now-abandoned enclave of Nan Madol, a group of 92 man-made islands off the shore of the Micronesian island of Pohnpei, is estimated to have been built around the year 500 A.D.

   4. The islanders say their ancestors quarried stone columns from a nearby island, where large basalt columns were formed by the cooling of molten lava.

   5. The structures of Nan Madol are remarkable for the sheer size of some of the stone "logs" or columns that were used to create the walls of the offshore community, and today anthropologists can only rely on the information of existing local people for clues about how Nan Madol was built.

The best order is

   A. 5 4 3 2 1
   B. 5 3 1 4 2
   C. 3 5 4 2 1
   D. 3 1 4 2 5

Question 23   23.____

  1. One of the most easily manipulated substances on earth, glass can be made into ceramic tiles that are composed of over 90% air.

  2. NASA's space shuttles are the first spacecraft ever designed to leave and re-enter the earth's atmosphere while remaining intact.

  3. These ceramic tiles are such effective insulators that when a tile emerges from the oven in which it was fired, it can be held safely in a person's hand by the edges while its interior still glows at a temperature well over 2000° F.

  4. Eventually, the engineers were led to a material that is as old as our most ancient civiliza-tionsglass.

  5. Because the temperature during atmospheric re-entry is so incredibly hot, it took NASA's engineers some time to find a substance capable of protecting the shuttles.

The best order is

    A. 5 2 1 3 4
    B. 2 5 4 1 3
    C. 2 3 1 2 5
    D. 5 4 3 1 2

Question 24   24.____

  1. The secret to teaching any parakeet to talk is patience, and the understanding that when a bird "talks," it is simply imitating what it hears, rather than putting ideas into words.

  2. You should stay just out of sight of the bird and repeat the phrase you want it to learn, for at least fifteen minutes every morning and evening.

  3. It is important to leave the bird without any words of encouragement or farewell; otherwise it might combine stray remarks or phrases, such as "Good night," with the phrase you are trying to teach it.

  4. For this reason, to train your bird to imitate your words you should keep it free of any dis-tractions, especially other noises, while you are giving it "lessons."

  5. After your repetition, you should quietly leave the bird alone for a while, to think over what it has just heard.

The best order is

    A. 1 4 2 5 3
    B. 1 2 4 3 5
    C. 3 2 1 5 4
    D. 3 1 5 4 2

Question 25

25._____

1. As a school approaches, fishermen from neighboring communities join their fishing boats together as a fleet, and string their gill nets together to make a huge fence that is held up by cork floats.
2. At a signal from the party leaders, or *nakura,* the family members pound the sides of the boats or beat the water with long poles, creating a sudden and deafening noise.
3. The fishermen work together to drag the trap into a half-circle that may reach 300 yards in diameter, and then the families move their boats to form the other half of the circle around the school of fish.
4. The school of fish flee from the commotion into the awaiting trap, where a final wall of net is thrown over the open end of the half-circle, securing the day's haul.
5. Indonesian people from the area around the Sulu islands live on the sea, in floating villages made of lashed-together or stilted homes, and make much of their living by fishing their home waters for migrating schools of snapper, scad, and other fish.

The best order is

A. 1 5 3 4 2
B. 1 2 4 3 5
C. 5 1 2 3 4
D. 5 1 3 2 4

KEY (CORRECT ANSWERS)

1.	D		11.	C
2.	D		12.	A
3.	B		13.	D
4.	A		14.	C
5.	C		15.	D
6.	C		16.	C
7.	D		17.	A
8.	D		18.	D
9.	A		19.	B
10.	B		20.	A

21.	A
22.	C
23.	B
24.	A
25.	D

PREPARING WRITTEN MATERIALS

EXAMINATION SECTION
TEST 1

DIRECTIONS: Each question consists of a sentence which may be classified appropriately under one of the following four categories:
- A. Incorrect because of faulty grammar or sentence structure;
- B. Incorrect because of faulty punctuation;
- C. Incorrect because of faulty capitalization;
- D. Correct.

Examine each sentence carefully. Then, in the space at the right, indicate the letter preceding the category which is the BEST of the four suggested above. Each incorrect sentence contains only one type of error. Consider a sentence correct if it contains no errors, although there may be other correct ways of expressing the same thought.

1. All the employees, in this office, are over twenty-one years old.   1.____

2. Neither the clerk nor the stenographer was able to explain what had happened.   2.____

3. Mr. Johnson did not know who he would assign to type the order.   3.____

4. Mr. Marshall called her to report for work on Saturday.   4.____

5. He might of arrived on time if the train had not been delayed.   5.____

6. Some employees on the other hand, are required to fill out these forms every month.   6.____

7. The supervisor issued special instructions to his subordinates to prevent their making errors.   7.____

8. Our supervisor Mr. Williams, expects to be promoted in about two weeks.   8.____

9. We were informed that prof. Morgan would attend the conference.   9.____

10. The clerks were assigned to the old building; the stenographers, to the new building.   10.____

11. The supervisor asked Mr. Smith and I to complete the work as quickly as possible.   11.____

12. He said, that before an employee can be permitted to leave, the report must be finished.   12.____

13. An adding machine, in addition to the three typewriters, are needed in the new office.   13.____

14. Having made many errors in her work, the supervisor asked the typist to be more careful.   14.____

15. "If you are given an assignment," he said, "you should begin work on it as quickly as possible."   15.____

16. All the clerks, including those who have been appointed recently are required to work on the new assignment.   16.____

17. The office manager asked each employee to work one Saturday a month. 17.____

18. Neither Mr. Smith nor Mr. Jones was able to finish his assignment on time. 18.____

19. The task of filing these cards is to be divided equally between you and he. 19.____

20. He is an employee whom we consider to be efficient. 20.____

21. I believe that the new employees are not as punctual as us. 21.____

22. The employees, working in this office, are to be congratulated for their work. 22.____

23. The delay in preparing the report was caused, in his opinion, by the lack of proper super-vision and coordination. 23.____

24. John Jones accidentally pushed the wrong button and then all the lights went out. 24.____

25. The investigator ought to of had the witness sign the statement. 25.____

KEY (CORRECT ANSWERS)

1.	B	11.	A
2.	D	12.	B
3.	A	13.	A
4.	C	14.	A
5.	A	15.	D
6.	B	16.	B
7.	D	17.	C
8.	B	18.	D
9.	C	19.	A
10.	D	20.	D

21.	A
22.	B
23.	D
24.	D
25.	A

TEST 2

Questions 1-10.

DIRECTIONS: Each of the following sentences may be classified under one of the following four options:
- A. Faulty; contains an error in grammar only
- B. Faulty; contains an error in spelling only
- C. Faulty; contains an error in grammar and an error in spelling
- D. Correct; contains no error in grammar or in spelling

Examine each sentence carefully to determine under which of the above four options it is BEST classified. Then, in the space at the right, write the letter preceding the option which is the best of the four listed above.

1. A recognized principle of good management is that an assignment should be given to whomever is best qualified to carry it out.   1._____

2. He considered it a privilege to be allowed to review and summarize the technical reports issued annually by your agency.   2._____

3. Because the warehouse was in an inaccessable location, deliveries of electric fixtures from the warehouse were made only in large lots.   3._____

4. Having requisitioned the office supplies, Miss Brown returned to her desk and resumed the computation of petty cash disbursements.   4._____

5. One of the advantages of this chemical solution is that records treated with it are not inflamable.   5._____

6. The complaint of this employee, in addition to the complaints of the other employees, were submitted to the grievance committee.   6._____

7. A study of the duties and responsibilities of each of the various categories of employees was conducted by an unprejudiced classification analyst. 7._____

8. Ties of friendship with this subordinate compels him to withold the censure that the subordinate deserves.   8._____

9. Neither of the agencies are affected by the decision to institute a program for rehabilitating physically handi-caped men and women.   9._____

10. The chairman stated that the argument between you and he was creating an intolerable situation.   10._____

Questions 11-25.

DIRECTIONS: Each of the following sentences may be classified under one of the following four options:

A. Correct
B. Sentence contains an error in spelling
C. Sentence contains an error in grammar
D. Sentence contains errors in both grammar and spelling.

11. He reported that he had had a really good time during his vacation although the farm was located in a very inaccessible portion of the country.   11.____

12. It looks to me like he has been fasinated by that beautiful painting.   12.____

13. We have permitted these kind of pencils to accumulate on our shelves, knowing we can sell them at a profit of five cents apiece any time we choose.   13.____

14. Believing that you will want an unexagerated estimate of the amount of business we can expect, I have made every effort to secure accurate figures.   14.____

15. Each and every man, woman and child in that untrameled wilderness carry guns for protection against the wild animals.   15.____

16. Although this process is different than the one to which he is accustomed, a good chemist will have no trouble.   16.____

17. Insensible to the fuming and fretting going on about him, the engineer continued to drive the mammoth dynamo to its utmost capacity.   17.____

18. Everyone had studied his lesson carefully and was consequently well prepared when the instructor began to discuss the fourth dimention.   18.____

19. I learned Johnny six new arithmetic problems this afternoon.   19.____

20. Athletics is urged by our most prominent citizens as the pursuit which will enable the younger generation to achieve that ideal of education, a sound mind in a sound body.   20.____

21. He did not see whoever was at the door very clearly but thinks it was the city tax appraiser.   21.____

22. He could not scarsely believe that his theories had been substantiated in this convincing fashion.   22.____

23. Although you have displayed great ingenuity in carrying out your assignments, the choice for the position still lies among Brown and Smith.   23.____

24. If they had have pleaded at the time that Smith was an accessory to the crime, it would have lessened the punishment.   24.____

25. It has proven indispensible in his compilation of the facts in the matter.   25.____

KEY (CORRECT ANSWERS)

1.	A		11.	A
2.	D		12.	D
3.	B		13.	C
4.	D		14.	B
5.	B		15.	D
6.	A		16.	C
7.	D		17.	A
8.	C		18.	B
9.	C		19.	C
10.	A		20.	A

21.	B
22.	D
23.	C
24.	D
25.	B

———

TEST 3

Questions 1-5.

DIRECTIONS: Questions 1 through 5 consist of sentences which may or may not contain errors in grammar or spelling or both. Sentences which do not contain errors in grammar or spelling or both are to be considered correct, even though there may be other correct ways of expressing the same thought. Examine each sentence carefully. Then, in the space at the right, write the letter of the answer which is the BEST of those suggested below:
  A. If the sentence is correct;
  B. If the sentence contains an error in spelling;
  C. If the sentence contains an error in grammar;
  D. If the sentence contains errors in both grammar and spelling.

1. Brown is doing fine although the work is irrevelant to his training. 1._____

2. The conference of sales managers voted to set its adjournment at one o'clock in order to give those present an opportunity to get rid of all merchandise. 2._____

3. He decided that in view of what had taken place at the hotel that he ought to stay and thank the benificent stranger who had rescued him from an embarassing situation. 3._____

4. Since you object to me criticizing your letter, I have no alternative but to consider you a mercenary scoundrel. 4._____

5. I rushed home ahead of schedule so that you will leave me go to the picnic with Mary. 5._____

Questions 6-15.

DIRECTIONS: Some of the following sentences contain an error in spelling, word usage, or sentence structure, or punctuation. Some sentences are correct as they stand although there may be other correct ways of expressing the same thought. All incorrect sentences contain only one error. Mark your answer to each question in the space at the right as follows:
  A. If the sentence has an error in spelling;
  B. If the sentence has an error in punctuation or capitalization;
  C. If the sentence has an error in word usage or sentence structure;
  D. If the sentence is correct.

6. Because the chairman failed to keep the participants from wandering off into irrelevant discussions, it was impossible to reach a consensus before the meeting was adjourned. 6._____

7. Certain employers have an unwritten rule that any applicant, who is over 55 years of age, is automatically excluded from consideration for any position whatsoever. 7._____

8. If the proposal to build schools in some new apartment buildings were to be accepted by the builders, one of the advantages that could be expected to result would be better communication between teachers and parents of schoolchildren. 8._____

9. In this instance, the manufacturer's violation of the law against deseptive packaging was discernible only to an experienced inspector. 9._____

10. The tenants' anger stemmed from the president's going to Washington to testify without consulting them first.   10.____

11. Did the president of this eminent banking company say; "We intend to hire and train a number of these disadvan-taged youths?"   11.____

12. In addition, today's confidential secretary must be knowledgable in many different areas: for example, she must know modern techniques for making travel arrangements for the executive.   12.____

13. To avoid further disruption of work in the offices, the protesters were forbidden from entering the building unless they had special passes.   13.____

14. A valuable secondary result of our training conferences is the opportunities afforded for management to observe the reactions of the participants.   14.____

15. Of the two proposals submitted by the committee, the first one is the best.   15.____

Questions 16-25.

DIRECTIONS: Each of the following sentences may be classified MOST appropriately under one of the following three categories:
  A. Faulty because of incorrect grammar
  B. Faulty because of incorrect punctuation
  C. Correct

Examine each sentence. Then, print the capital letter preceding the BEST choice of the three suggested above. All incorrect sentences contain only one type of error. Consider a sentence correct if it contains none of the types of errors mentioned, even though there may be other ways of expressing the same thought.

16. He sent the notice to the clerk who you hired yesterday.   16.____

17. It must be admitted, however that you were not informed of this change.   17.____

18. Only the employees who have served in this grade for at least two years are eligible for promotion.   18.____

19. The work was divided equally between she and Mary.   19.____

20. He thought that you were not available at that time.   20.____

21. When the messenger returns; please give him this package.   21.____

22. The new secretary prepared, typed, addressed, and delivered, the notices.   22.____

23. Walking into the room, his desk can be seen at the rear.   23.____

24. Although John has worked here longer than she, he produces a smaller amount of work.   24.____

25. She said she could of typed this report yesterday.   25.____

KEY (CORRECT ANSWERS)

1.	D	11.	B
2.	A	12.	A
3.	D	13.	C
4.	C	14.	D
5.	C	15.	C
6.	A	16.	A
7.	B	17.	B
8.	D	18.	C
9.	A	19.	A
10.	D	20.	C

21.	B
22.	B
23.	A
24.	C
25.	A

TEST 4

Questions 1-5.

DIRECTIONS: Each of the following sentences may be classified MOST appropriately under one of the following three categories:
A. Faulty because of incorrect grammar
B. Faulty because of incorrect punctuation
C. Correct

Examine each sentence. Then, print the capital letter preceding the BEST choice of the three suggested above. All incorrect sentences contain only one type of error. Consider a sentence correct if it contains none of the types of errors mentioned, even though there may be other correct ways of expressing the same thought.

1. Neither one of these procedures are adequate for the efficient performance of this task.   1.____

2. The typewriter is the tool of the typist; the cash register, the tool of the cashier.   2.____

3. "The assignment must be completed as soon as possible" said the supervisor.   3.____

4. As you know, office handbooks are issued to all new employees.   4.____

5. Writing a speech is sometimes easier than to deliver it before an audience.   5.____

Questions 6-15.

DIRECTIONS: Each statement given in Questions 6 through 15 contains one of the faults of English usage listed below. For each, choose from the options listed the MAJOR fault contained.
A. The statement is not a complete sentence.
B. The statement contains a word or phrase that is redundant.
C. The statement contains a long, less commonly used word when a shorter, more direct word would be acceptable.
D. The statement contains a colloquial expression that normally is avoided in business writing.

6. The fact that this activity will afford an opportunity to meet your group.   6.____

7. Do you think that the two groups can join together for next month's meeting?   7.____

8. This is one of the most exciting new innovations to be introduced into our college.   8.____

9. We expect to consummate the agenda before the meeting ends tomorrow at noon.   9.____

10. While this seminar room is small in size, we think we can use it.   10.____

11. Do you think you can make a modification in the date of the Budget Committee meeting?   11.____

12. We are cognizant of the problem but we think we can ameliorate the situation.   12.____

13. Shall I call you around three on the day I arrive in the City?   13.____

14. Until such time that we know precisely that the students will be present.   14.____

15. The consensus of opinion of all the members present is reported in the minutes.   15.____

Questions 16-25.

DIRECTIONS: For each of Questions 16 through 25, select from the options given below the MOST applicable choice.
      A.   The sentence is correct.
      B.   The sentence contains a spelling error only.
      C.   The sentence contains an English grammar error only.
      D.   The sentence contains both a spelling error and an English grammar error.

16. Every person in the group is going to do his share.   16.____

17. The man who we selected is new to this University.   17.____

18. She is the older of the four secretaries on the two staffs that are to be combined.   18.____

19. The decision has to be made between him and I.   19.____

20. One of the volunteers are too young for this complecated task, don't you think?   20.____

21. I think your idea is splindid and it will improve this report considerably.   21.____

22. Do you think this is an exagerated account of the behavior you and me observed this morning?   22.____

23. Our supervisor has a clear idea of excelence.   23.____

24. How many occurences were verified by the observers?   24.____

25. We must complete the typing of the draft of the questionaire by noon tomorrow.   25.____

———

KEY (CORRECT ANSWERS)

1.	A		11.	C
2.	C		12.	C
3.	B		13.	D
4.	C		14.	A
5.	A		15.	B
6.	A		16.	A
7.	B		17.	C
8.	B		18.	C
9.	C		19.	C
10.	B		20.	D

21.	B
22.	D
23.	B
24.	B
25.	B

———

INTERPRETING STATISTICAL DATA
GRAPHS, CHARTS AND TABLES

TEST 1

DIRECTIONS: Each question or incomplete statement is followed by several suggested answers or completions. Select the one that BEST answers the question or completes the statement. *PRINT THE LETTER OF THE CORRECT ANSWER IN THE SPACE AT THE RIGHT.*

Questions 1-5.

DIRECTIONS: Questions 1 through 5 are to be answered SOLELY on the basis of the following table.

ANNUAL SALARIES PAID TO SELECTED CLERICAL TITLES IN FIVE MAJOR CITIES IN 2012 AND 2014				

2014

	Clerk	Typist	Steno	Legal Steno	Computer Operator
Newton	$33,900	$34,800	$36,300	$43,800	$35,400
Barton	$32,400	$34,200	$35,400	$43,500	$34,200
Phelton	$32,400	$32,400	$34,200	$42,000	$33,000
Washburn	$33,600	$34,800	$35,400	$43,800	$34,800
Biltmore	$33,000	$34,200	$35,100	$43,500	$34,500

2012

	Clerk	Typist	Steno	Legal Steno	Computer Operator
Newtown	$31,800	$33,600	$35,400	$41,400	$34,500
Barton	$30,000	$31,500	$33,000	$39,600	$31,500
Phelton	$29,400	$30,600	$31,800	$37,800	$31,200
Washburn	$30,600	$32,400	$33,600	$40,200	$32,400
Biltmore	$30,000	$31,800	$33,000	$39,600	$32,100

1. Assume that the value of the fringe benefits offered to clerical employees in 2014 amounted to 14% of their annual salaries in Newton, 17% in Barton, 18% in Phelton, 15% in Washburn, and 16% in Biltmore.
   The total cost of employing a computer operator for 2014 was GREATEST in

   A. Newtown   B. Barton   C. Phelton   D. Washburn

   1.____

2. During negotiations for their 2015 contract, the stenographers of Biltmore are demanding that their rate of pay be fixed at 85% of the legal stenographer salary.
   If this demand is granted and if the legal stenographer salary increases by 7% in 2015, the 2015 stenographer salary will be MOST NEARLY

   A. $36,972   B. $37,560   C. $39,564   D. $40,020

   2.____

3. Of the following, the GREATEST percentage increase in salary from 2012 to 2014 was gained by

    3.____

    A. clerks in Newtown
    B. stenographers in Barton
    C. legal stenographers in Washburn
    D. computer operators in Biltmore

4. The title which achieved the SMALLEST average percentage increase in salary from 2012 to 2014 was

    4.____

    A. clerk   B. typist
    C. stenographer   D. legal stenographer

5. Assume that, in 2014, clerks accounted for 60% of the clerical work force in Barton. The clerical work force consists of 140 employees. In 2012, the clerks accounted for 65% of the clerical work force in Barton. The clerical work force then consisted of 120 employees.
The difference between the 2012 and 2014 payroll for clerks in Barton is MOST NEARLY

    5.____

    A. $120,000   B. $240,000   C. $360,000   D. $480,000

KEY (CORRECT ANSWERS)

    1. A
    2. C
    3. C
    4. C
    5. C

TEST 2

Questions 1-9.

DIRECTIONS: Questions 1 through 9 are to be answered SOLELY on the basis of the facts given in the table below, which contains certain information about employees in a city bureau.

NAME	TITLE	AGE	ANNUAL SALARY	YEARS OF SERVICE	EXAMINATION RATING
Jones	Clerk	34	$20,400	10	82
Smith	Stenographer	25	19,200	2	72
Black	Typist	19	14,400	1	71
Brown	Stenographer	36	25,200	12	88
Thomas	Accountant	49	41,200	21	91
Gordon	Clerk	31	30,000	8	81
Johnson	Stenographer	26	26,400	5	75
White	Accountant	53	36,000	30	90
Spencer	Clerk	42	27,600	19	85
Taylor	Typist	24	21,600	5	74
Simpson	Accountant	37	50,000	11	87
Reid	Typist	20	12,000	2	72
Fulton	Accountant	55	55,000	31	100
Chambers	Clerk	22	15,600	4	75
Calhoun	Stenographer	48	28,800	16	80

RECORD OF EMPLOYEES IN A CITY BUREAU

1. The name of the employee whose salary would be the middle one if all the salaries were ranked in order of magnitude is

   A. White   B. Johnson   C. Brown   D. Spencer

1.____

2. The combined monthly salary of all the stenographers EXCEEDS the combined monthly salary of all the clerks by

   A. $6,000   B. $500   C. $22,800   D. $600

2.____

3. The age of the employee who received the HIGHEST rating in the examination among those who have less than 10 years of service is _____ years.

   A. 22   B. 31   C. 55   D. 34

3.____

4. The average examination rating of those employees who had 15 years of service or more as compared with the average examination rating of those employees who had 5 years of service or less is MOST NEARLY _____ points _____.

   A. 16; greater   B. 7; greater
   C. 10; less   D. 25; greater

4.____

5. The name of the youngest employee whose monthly salary is more than $1,000 per month and who has more than one year of service is

   A. Reid   B. Black   C. Chambers   D. Taylor

5.____

6. The name of the employee who received an examination rating of over 85%, who has more than 15 years of service, and who earns a yearly salary of more than $25,000 but less than $40,000 is

   A. Thomas   B. Spencer   C. Calhoun   D. White

6.____

7. The annual salary of the HIGHEST paid stenographer is

    A. more than twice as great as the salary of the youngest employee
    B. greater than the salary of the oldest typist but not as great as the salary of the oldest clerk
    C. greater than the salary of the highest paid typist but not as great as the salary of the lowest paid accountant
    D. less than the combined salaries of the two youngest typists

7.____

8. The number of employees whose annual salary is more than $15,600 but less than $28,800 and who have at least 5 years of service is

    A. 11   B. 8   C. 6   D. 5

8.____

9. Of the following, it would be MOST accurate to state that the

    A. youngest employee is lowest with respect to number of years of service, examination rating, and salary
    B. oldest employee is highest with respect to number of years of service, examination rating, but not with respect to salary
    C. annual salary of the youngest clerk is $1,200 more than the annual salary of the youngest typist and $2,400 less than the annual salary of the youngest stenographer
    D. difference in age between the youngest and oldest typist is less than one-fourth the difference in age between the youngest and oldest stenographer

9.____

KEY (CORRECT ANSWERS)

1. B
2. B
3. B
4. A
5. C
6. D
7. C
8. D
9. D

TEST 3

Questions 1-10.

DIRECTIONS: Questions 1 through 10 are to be answered SOLELY on the basis of the Personnel Record of Division X shown below.

| | | | | No. of Days Absent | | |
| | Bureau In | | Annual | On Vaca- | On Sick | No. of Times |
Employee	Which Employed	Title	Salary	tion	Leave	Late
Abbott	Mail	Clerk	$31,200	18	0	1
Barnes	Mail	Clerk	25,200	25	3	7
Davis	Mail	Typist	24,000	21	9	2
Adams	Payroll	Accountant	42,500	10	0	2
Bell	Payroll	Bookkeeper	31,200	23	2	5
Duke	Payroll	Clerk	27,600	24	4	3
Gross	Payroll	Clerk	21,600	12	5	7
Lane	Payroll	Stenographer	26,400	19	16	20
Reed	Payroll	Typist	22,800	15	11	11
Arnold	Record	Clerk	32,400	6	15	9
Cane	Record	Clerk	24,500	14	3	4
Fay	Record	Clerk	21,100	20	0	4
Hale	Record	Typist	25,200	18	2	7
Baker	Supply	Clerk	30,000	20	3	2
Clark	Supply	Clerk	27,600	25	6	5
Ford	Supply	Typist	22,800	25	4	22

DIVISION X
PERSONNEL RECORD - CURRENT YEAR

1. The percentage of the total number of employees who are clerks is MOST NEARLY   1.____

   A. 25%   B. 33%   C. 38%   D. 56%

2. Of the following employees, the one who receives a monthly salary of $2,100 is   2.____

   A. Barnes   B. Gross   C. Reed   D. Clark

3. The difference between the annual salary of the highest paid clerk and that of the lowest   3.____
   paid clerk is

   A. $6,000   B. $8,400   C. $11,300   D. $20,900

4. The number of employees receiving more than $25,000 a year but less than $40,000 a   4.____
   year is

   A. 6   B. 9   C. 12   D. 15

5. The TOTAL annual salary of the employees of the Mail Bureau is _____ the total annual   5.____
   salary of the employees of the _____.

   A. one-half of; Payroll Bureau
   B. less than; Record Bureau by $21,600
   C. equal to; Supply Bureau
   D. less than; Payroll Bureau by $71,600

6. The average annual salary of the employees who are not clerks is MOST NEARLY   6.___

    A. $23,700   B. $25,450   C. $26,800   D. $27,850

7. If all the employees were given a 10% increase in pay, the annual salary of Lane would   7.___
then be

    A. *greater* than that of Barnes by $1,320
    B. *less* than that of Bell by $4,280
    C. *equal* to that of Clark
    D. *greater* than that of Ford by $3,600

8. Of the clerks who earned less than $30,000 a year, the one who was late the FEWEST   8.___
number of times was late _____ time(s).

    A. 1   B. 2   C. 3   D. 4

9. The bureau in which the employees were late the FEWEST number of times on an aver-   9.___
age is the _____ Bureau.

    A. Mail   B. Payroll   C. Record   D. Supply

10. The MOST accurate of the following statements is that   10.___

    A. Reed was late more often than any other typist
    B. Bell took more time off for vacation than any other employee earning $30,000 or
more annually
    C. of the typists, Ford was the one who was absent the fewest number of times
because of sickness
    D. three clerks took no time off because of sickness

KEY (CORRECT ANSWERS)

    1. D
    2. A
    3. C
    4. B
    5. C
    6. D
    7. A
    8. C
    9. A
  10. B

TEST 4

Questions 1-10.

DIRECTIONS: Questions 1 through 10 are to be answered SOLELY on the basis of the Weekly Payroll Record shown below of Bureau X in a public agency. In answering these questions, note that gross weekly salary is the salary before deductions have been made; take-home pay is the amount remaining after all indicated weekly deductions have been made from the gross weekly salary. In answering questions involving annual amounts, compute on the basis of 52 weeks per year.

			Gross Weekly Salary (Before Deductions)	Weekly Deductions From Gross Salary		
Unit In Which Employed	Employee	Title		Medical Insurance	Income Tax	Pension System
Accounting	Allen	Accountant	$950	$14.50	$125.00	$53.20
Accounting	Barth	Bookkeeper	720	19.00	62.00	40.70
Accounting	Keller	Clerk	580	6.50	82.00	33.10
Accounting	Peters	Typist	560	6.50	79.00	35.30
Accounting	Simons	Stenographer	610	14.50	64.00	37.80
Information	Brown	Clerk	560	13.00	56.00	42.20
Information	Smith	Clerk	590	14.50	61.00	58.40
Information	Turner	Typist	580	13.00	59.00	62.60
Information	Williams	Stenographer	620	19.00	44.00	69.40
Mail	Conner	Clerk	660	13.00	74.00	55.40
Mail	Farrell	Typist	540	6.50	75.00	34.00
Mail	Johnson	Stenographer	580	19.00	36.00	37.10
Records	Dillon	Clerk	640	6.50	94.00	58.20
Records	Martin	Clerk	540	19.00	29.00	50.20
Records	Standish	Typist	620	14.50	67.00	60.10
Records	Wilson	Stenographer	690	6.50	101.00	75.60

BUREAU X — WEEKLY PAYROLL PERIOD

1. Dillon's annual take-home pay is MOST NEARLY

    A. $25,000   B. $27,000   C. $31,000   D. $33,000

1.____

2. The difference between Turner's gross annual salary and his annual take-home pay is MOST NEARLY

    A. $3,000   B. $5,000   C. $7,000   D. $9,000

2.____

3. Of the following, the employee whose weekly take-home pay is CLOSEST to that of Keller's is

    A. Peters   B. Brown   C. Smith   D. Turner

3.____

4. The average gross annual salary of the typists is

    A. less than $27,500
    B. more than $27,500 but less than $30,000
    C. more than $30,000 but less than $32,500
    D. more than $32,500

4.____

5. The average gross weekly salary of the stenographers EXCEEDS the gross weekly sal-   5.____
   ary of the clerks by

    A. $20   B. $30   C. $40   D. $50

6. Of the following employees in the Accounting Unit, the one who pays the HIGHEST per-   6.____
   centage of his gross weekly salary for the Pension System is

    A. Barth   B. Keller   C. Peters   D. Simons

7. For all of the Accounting Unit employees, the total annual deductions for Medical Insur-   7.____
   ance are less than the total annual deductions for the Pension System by MOST
   NEARLY

    A. $6,000   B. $7,000   C. $8,000   D. $9,000

8. Of the following, the employee whose total weekly deductions are MOST NEARLY 27%   8.____
   of his gross weekly salary is

    A. Barth   B. Brown   C. Martin   D. Wilson

9. The total amount of the gross weekly salaries of all the employees in the Records Unit is   9.____
   MOST NEARLY

    A. 95% of the total amount of the gross weekly salaries of all the employees in the
          Information Unit
    B. 10% greater than the total amount of the gross weekly salaries of all the employ-
          ees in the Mail Unit
    C. 75% of the total amount of the gross weekly salaries of all the employees in the
          Accounting Unit
    D. four times as great as the total amount deducted weekly for tax for all the employ-
          ees in the Records Unit

10. For the employees in the Information Unit, the AVERAGE weekly deductions for Income   10.____
    Tax _____ the average weekly deduction for _____.

    A. exceeds; Income Tax for the employees in the Records Unit
    B. is less than; the Pension System for the employees in the Mail Unit
    C. exceeds; Income Tax for the employees in the Accounting Unit
    D. is less than; the Pension System for the employees in the Records Unit

KEY (CORRECT ANSWERS)

1. A
2. C
3. C
4. B
5. B
6. C
7. B
8. D
9. C
10. D

———

TEST 5

DIRECTIONS: Questions 1 through 9 are to be answered SOLELY on the basis of the following information.

Assume that the following rules for computing service ratings are to be used experimen-
tally in determining the service ratings of seven permanent city employees. (Note that these
rules are hypothetical and are NOT to be confused with the existing method of computing service ratings for city employees.) The personnel record of each of these seven employees is
given in Table II. You are to determine the answer to each of the questions on the basis of the
rules given below for computing service ratings and the data contained in the personnel
records of these seven employees.

All computations should be made as of the close of the rating period ending March 31,
2017.

Service Rating
The service rating of each permanent competitive class employee shall be computed by
adding the following three scores: (1) a basic score, (2) the employee's seniority score, and
(3) the employee's efficiency score.

Seniority Score
An employee's seniority score shall be computed by crediting him with 1/2% per year for
each year of service starting with the date of the employee's entrance as a permanent
employee into the competitive class, up to a maximum of 15 years (7 1/2%).

A residual fractional period of eight months or more shall be considered as a full year
and credited with 1/2%. A residual fraction of from four to, but not including, eight months
shall be considered as a half-year and credited with 1/4%. A residual fraction of less than four
months shall receive no credit in the seniority score.

For example, a person who entered the competitive class as a permanent employee on
August 1, 2014 would, as of March 31, 2017, be credited with a seniority score of 1 1/2% for
his 2 years and 8 months of service.

Efficiency Score
An employee's efficiency score shall be computed by adding the annual efficiency ratings
received by him during his service in his present position. (Where there are negative efficiency ratings, such ratings shall be subtracted from the sum of the positive efficiency ratings.) An employee's annual efficiency rating shall be based on the grade he receives from
his supervisor for his work performance during the annual efficiency rating period.

Basic Score
A basic score of 70% shall be given to each employee upon permanent appointment to a
competitive class position.

An employee shall receive a grade of A for performing work of the highest quality and
shall be credited with an efficiency rating of plus (+) 3%. An employee shall receive a grade of
F for performing work of the lowest quality and shall receive an efficiency rating of minus (-)
2%. Table I, entitled BASIS FOR DETERMINING ANNUAL EFFICIENCY RATINGS, lists the
six grades of work performance with their equivalent annual efficiency ratings. Table I also

lists the efficiency ratings to be assigned for service in a position for less than a year during the annual efficiency rating period.

The annual efficiency rating period shall run from April 1 to March 31, inclusive.

TABLE I – BASIS FOR DETERMINING ANNUAL EFFICIENCY RATINGS				
			Annual Efficiency Rating for Service in a Position For:		
Quality of Work Performed	Grade Assigned	8 months to a full year	At least 4 months but less than 8 months	Less than 4 months
Highest	A	+3%	+1 1/2%	0%
Good	B	+2%	+1%	0%
Standard	C	+1%	+1/2%	0%
Substandard	D	0%	0%	0%
Poor	E	-1%	-4%	0%
Lowest	F	-2%	-1%	0%

Appointment or Promotion During an Efficiency Rating Period

An employee who has been appointed or promoted during an efficiency rating period shall receive for that period an efficiency rating only for work performed by him during the portion of the period that he served in the position to which he was appointed or promoted. His efficiency rating for the period shall be determined in accordance with Table I.

Sample Computation of Service Rating

John Smith entered the competitive class as a permanent employee on December 1, 2012 and was promoted to his present position as a Clerk, Grade 3, on November 1, 2015. As a Clerk, Grade 3, he received a grade of B for work performed during the five-month period extending from November 1, 2015 to March 31, 2016 and a grade of C for work performed during the full annual period extending from April 1, 2016 to March 31, 2017.

On the basis of the RULES FOR COMPUTING SERVICE RATINGS, John Smith should be credited with:

70%   Basic Score
2 1/4%. Seniority Score - for 4 years and 4 months of service (from 12/1/12 to 3/31/17)
2%   Efficiency Score - for 5 months of B service and a full _____ year of C service
74 1/4%

TABLE II			
PERSONNEL RECORD OF SEVEN PERMANENT			
COMPETITIVE CLASS EMPLOYEES			

Employee	Present Position	Date of Appointment or Promotion To Present Position	Date of Entry as Permanent Employee in Competitive Class
Allen	Clerk, Gr. 5	6-1-13	7-1-00
Brown	Clerk, Gr. 4	1-1-15	7-1-17
Cole	Clerk, Gr. 3	9-1-13	11-1-10
Fox	Clerk, Gr. 3	10-1-13	9-1-08
Green	Clerk, Gr. 2	12-1-11	12-1-11
Hunt	Clerk, Gr. 2	7-1-12	7-1-12
Kane	Steno, Gr. 3	11-16-14	3-1-11

GRADES RECEIVED ANNUALLY FOR WORK PERFORMED IN PRESENT POSITION

Employee	4-1-11 to 3-31-12	4-1-12 to 3-31-13	4-1-13 to 3-31-14	4-1-14 to 3-31-15	4-1-15 to 3-31-16	4-1-16 to 3-31-17
Allen			C*	C	B	C
Brown				C*	C	B
Cole			A*	B	C	C
Fox			C*	C	D	C
Green	C*	D	C	D	C	C
Hunt		C*	C	E	C	C
Kane				B*	B	C

EXPLANATORY NOTES:
* Served in present position for less than a full year during this rating period. (Note date of appointment, or promotion, to present position.)
All seven employees have served continuously as permanent employees since their entry into the competitive class.

Questions 1 through 9 refer to the employees listed in Table II. You are to answer these questions SOLELY on the basis of the preceding RULES FOR COMPUTING SERVICE RATINGS and on the information concerning these seven employees given in Table II. You are reminded that all computations are to be made as of the close of the rating period ending March 31, 2017. Candidates may find it helpful to arrange their computations on their scratch paper in an orderly manner since the computations for one question may also be utilized in answering another question.

1. The seniority score of Allen is

    A. 7 1/2%   B. 8 1/2%   C. 8%   D. 8 1/4%

2. The seniority score of Fox EXCEEDS that of Cole by

    A. 1 1/2%   B. 2%   C. 1%   D. 3/4%

3. The seniority score of Brown is

    A. *equal* to Hunt's   B. *twice* Hunt's
    C. *move* than Hunt's by 1 1/2%   D. *less* than by Hunt's by 1/2%

1.____

2.____

3.____

4. Green's efficiency score is

    A. *twice* that of Kane
    B. *equal* to that of Kane
    C. *less* than Kane's by 1/2%
    D. *less* than Kane's by 1%

4.____

5. Of the following employees, the one who has the LOWEST efficiency score is

    A. Brown   B. Fox   C. Hunt   D. Kane

5.____

6. A comparison of Hunt's efficiency score with his seniority score reveals that his efficiency score is

    A. *less* than his seniority score by 1/2%
    B. *less* than his seniority score by 3/4%
    C. *equal* to his seniority score
    D. *greater* than his seniority score by 1/2%

6.____

7. Fox's service rating is

    A. 72 1/2%   B. 74%   C. 76 1/2%   D. 76 3/4%

7.____

8. Brown's service rating is

    A. less than 78%   B. 78%
    C. 78 1/4%   D. more than 78 1/4%

8.____

9. Cole's service rating EXCEEDS Kane's by

    A. less than 2%   B. 2%
    C. 2 1/4%   D. more than 2 1/4%

9.____

KEY (CORRECT ANSWERS)

    1. A
    2. C
    3. B
    4. C
    5. B
    6. D
    7. D
    8. B
    9. A

CPSIA information can be obtained
at www.ICGtesting.com
Printed in the USA
LVHW022056171219
640814LV00022B/467